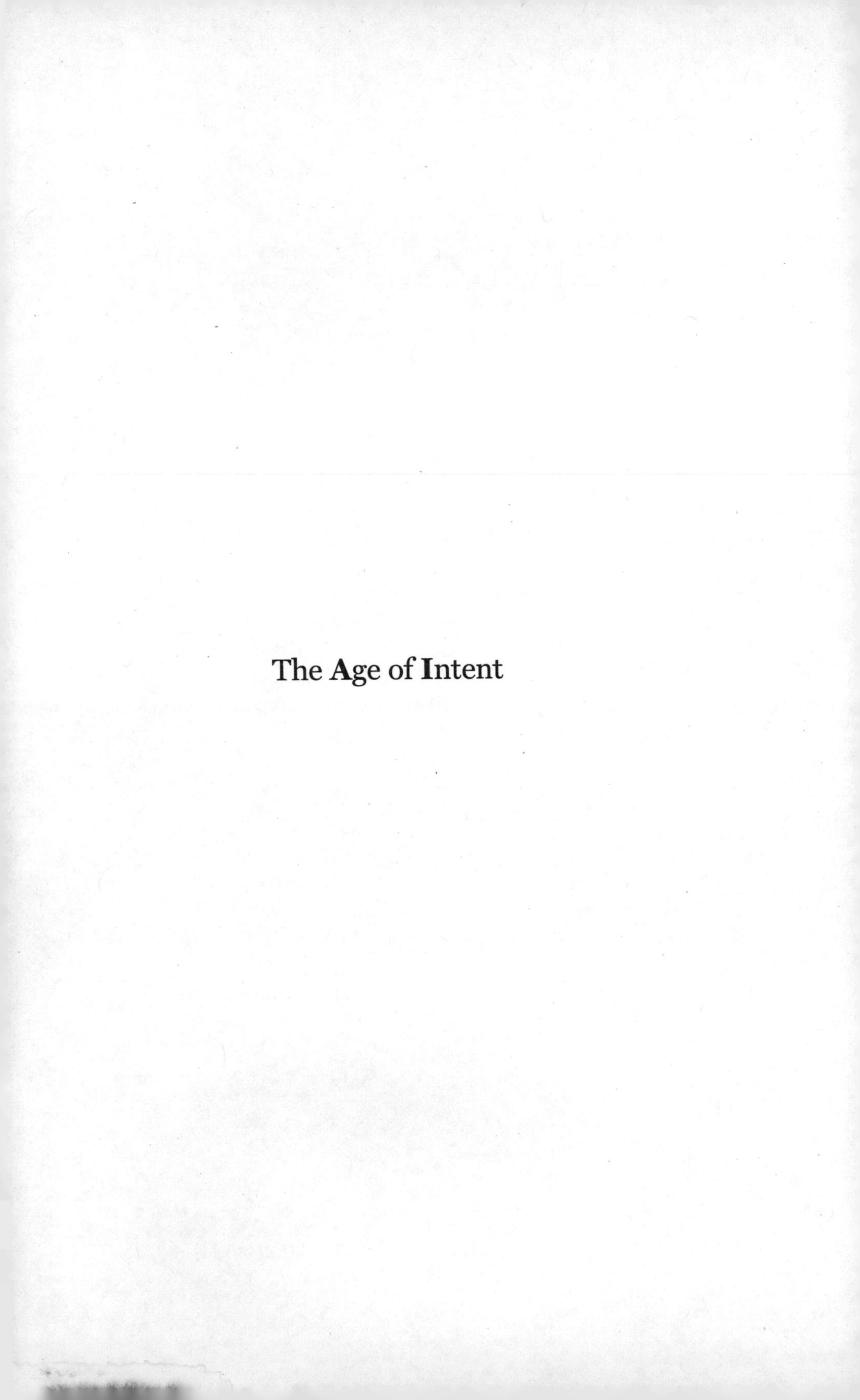

The Age of Intent

THE AGE OF INTENT

Using **Artificial Intelligence** to Deliver a Superior Customer Experience

P.V. KANNAN
with Josh Bernoff

www.amplifypublishing.com

The Age of Intent: Using Artificial Intelligence to Deliver a Superior Customer Experience

For more information, please contact:
Mascot Books
620 Herndon Parkway #320
Herndon, VA 20170
info@mascotbooks.com

Library of Congress Control Number: 2019933073
CPSIA Code: PRFRE0319A
ISBN-13: 978-1-64307-240-1

Printed in Canada

To the people of [24]7.ai
who work every day to make
the impossible possible.

CONTENTS

Foreword

HAVE YOUR BOT CALL MY BOT

One reason I pay close attention to technology, even though I am a foreign affairs columnist for the *New York Times*, is that I've learned over the years that whatever can be done, will be done. The only question is whether it will be done by you or to you. But just don't think it won't be done. I have also learned that bad guys are always early adopters; they live on the edge and tend to have fewer resources, so they're very quick and imaginative at finding new ways to bend new technologies to their ends. What P.V. Kannan is telling us in this new book, *The Age of Intent*, is about some new and important things that can be done and therefore will be done very soon—that many of us had not yet fully grasped—in the realm of people being able to converse with machines. It will have a profound impact on business, education, and, yes, crime.

As P.V. summarizes it, once people "*can* talk to devices and

get answers, they *will* talk to devices to get answers. If they're talking, then companies will want to be there to provide the answers they're looking for. It's faster, it's easier, and it's cheaper than today's customer service channels." And if this is where the next leap in technology is headed, then bad guys will be there as well. That is why this book should have your attention—whether you're a technologist, a CEO, a job seeker, an investor, or a policeman. It's defining one of the next big things coming down the information technology highway that will impact how we live, work, interact, buy, sell, and steal.

How did we get here? I think of it in terms of three giant steps from the late 1990s until today—and P.V.'s company, [24]7.ai, lived and transformed itself through all three steps.

I first met P.V. on a visit to Bangalore, India, in February 2004—the world capital of outsourcing—to do a documentary on outsourcing for the *New York Times* and Discovery. His company, which back then was just called 24/7 Customer—without the AI—helped to pioneer the call center revolution in India. It focused on training human agents, down to their accents, to respond to and anticipate the demands of other human beings calling in from all over the world to different companies' service and sales lines. P.V.'s human agents, mostly young Indian engineers, answered the phones and provided the services, advice, and sales pitches on behalf of those companies—all from Bangalore.

My visit to 24/7 Customer—and to other companies in Bangalore, such as Infosys—inspired me to write a book about the then-new technology platform aborning around the year 2000. It was called *The World Is Flat*. Technology moves up in steps: a set of technologies come together, they create a new set of capabilities, these proliferate and eventually give birth to a new set of technologies and a new platform—a step up.

The platform that had emerged in the early 2000s, a big step up, was one that enabled more people in more places to suddenly

compete, connect, and collaborate with more other people in more ways on more days for less money and with greater ease than ever before. I argued that what was unique about that platform was that it was, in effect, flattening the world—bringing hundreds of millions of people into the global collaboration network who never imagined being able to participate there before.

That particular step up in technology was dominated by breakthroughs in connectivity, particularly fiber optics, satellites, and the internet. And together they made connectivity fast, free, easy for you, and ubiquitous. Suddenly I could touch people I could never touch before and be touched by people who could never touch me before. The world got flat.

I believe that around 2007—when the first iPhone was released—we stepped up to another new platform, thanks to the emergence of big data, smartphones, broadband, Facebook, Twitter, Android, Hadoop, and "the cloud"—virtually all of which emerged in the same year, 2007. This new platform was biased toward complexity. New advances in software, storage capacity, software-enabling networking, search algorithms, and hardware combined to put grease into everything by abstracting away all the complexity and reducing it all to one touch on a smartphone.

With one light little touch on that phone in my pocket, I could rent a home in Bali on Airbnb, get a loan from PayPal, buy a basketful of goods on Amazon, split the dinner bill with my friends on Venmo, and page a taxi, direct a taxi, pay a taxi, rate a taxi, and be rated by a taxi on Uber. Every company had to build its apps and optimize its websites for mobile viewing and one-touch problem-solving, banking, news-reading, and millions of other things that used to take so much more time and effort. When all that complexity got abstracted into one touch, well, the world got fast.

Somewhere around 2015–2016, I believe we leapt up to another new platform. And it's the foundation of this book. This new platform was built by taking all the things that had made the world

flat and fast and amplifying them to also make the world smart.

That is to say, somewhere around 2015–2016, big data got really big, broadband got really broad, algorithms got really sophisticated about sorting unstructured data, and the cloud got really enormous and could hold massive amounts of that data—so artificial intelligence got really, really intelligent by training on all that data.

All of a sudden, Google's search engine could not only find anything you were looking for, but it could also intuit what you were looking for and what you would look for next—and even how you would finish your sentence in a search request. The bank's website not only could help you access your account on your own and enable you to make deposits or withdrawals or transfers, it could intuit a whole set of much deeper banking interactions you might want to make—or even grant you a loan based on predictive analytics—and do it all without any, or with minimal, human intervention by bank staff.

And best of all, we could begin to do all of that with no touch. Voice recognition technology and text interpretation technology became so good that what P.V. calls "virtual agents"—not all those young Indian kids—could answer the phone and handle many more queries and respond in a computer-generated voice or a computer-written text.

This new era is all about what can be done for you—not just by you—with no touch or minimal texting. It does so by using conversational interfaces powered by artificial intelligence that can understand your intent and respond just by hearing your voice or reading your text message. The ability of machines to discern and anticipate human intent is about to become fast, free, easy for the company you're interacting with, mobile, invisible, and ubiquitous. It is going to make the world flatter, faster, and smarter than ever before. Machines will be able to deliver deep insights with no touch.

I like how P.V. describes this moment: "You need to know just

when the fantasy turns to reality . . . The moment for virtual agents is now. . . . Computer systems inside companies have a lot of information about you and about the world. Based on knowing who is calling, where you are, what time of day it is, what the weather is, and a lot of other information—*based on context*—a virtual agent can rapidly identify what you are looking for . . . Virtual agents represent an inflection point—a rare opportunity to reduce costs and improve customer experience at the same time."

As noted, the first two big platforms of the internet age were built on websites and then mobile apps—with you navigating by yourself and for yourself. Now we will do it with virtual agents helping you to navigate yourself and navigating for you by anticipating where you want to go next. The companies that master this new platform the fastest will be the ones to overtake their competitors. Just don't think this new platform isn't coming. You only have to look at the explosive growth of Alexa, Siri, Google Assistant, and text messaging platforms like Facebook Messenger, WhatsApp, and WeChat to see what is barreling down the information technology highway.

As P.V. predicts, "Right now, people's impression of your brand has a lot to do with what they see on your mobile site. But as the conversation-first future arrives the [effectiveness of your] bot will be how people perceive your brand."

I came to better understand not only this new platform by reading this book but also the whole new language that this age of intent has spawned. As a foreign policy specialist, I always thought "containment" referred to the US policy toward the Soviet Union in the Cold War. P.V. has taught me that in the age of intent, "containment" is the term used by people in his industry when a virtual agent is able to solve a problem on its own without having to hand it over to a human agent. The percentage of calls that can be handled entirely by a chatbot, a virtual agent, constitutes your company's "containment rate."

I also learned the new term "conversational commerce," which refers to companies that use virtual agents to complete sales. And then there is my favorite new term: "customer journey analytics," known in the business as "CJA." CJA constitutes the analytical insights that companies derive by studying the data of how tens of thousands of customers journey by voice or text across their websites in their interactions with humans or virtual agents. The richer your CJA, the better trained your virtual agents become to understand and anticipate the intent of your customers—and therefore the more effective they become at solving your problems without a human or at converting queries into new products or services.

As such, a conversation-first strategy will be required by all companies, just as a mobile-first strategy was after the advent of the smartphone. And that means a whole new set of careers. As P.V. notes, "The visual designers who are best at mobile app design *aren't* the best at conversational design. Mobile designers focus on using screen elements to get you a limited set of answers instantly. Conversational designers, by contrast, need to recognize hundreds or thousands of intents and create dialogue appropriate for them." So, mom and dad, don't be surprised when your kid comes home from college and announces that they've decided to become a "conversational script writer."

By the way, the companies that improve and mine these conversational interactions with their customers the fastest will gain a huge advantage. "When you have a complete record of all your customers' intents over time," notes P.V., "you can map out their journeys and potential future relationship with your company. Every conversation is a communication generating data that your competitors are missing out on. And as a result, every conversation will improve the strength of connections with these customers."

This will also change the work of nonmachines—also known as "human beings." They will need more empathy and more granular knowledge of corporate systems and policies to handle all

the exceptions that the machine can't handle. They will be the ones pushing out the frontier for the next level of questions the machines need to be programmed to answer. Their job will be to tweak the virtual agents to make them steadily smarter.

As this improves over time, many people will surely have their own personal bot that knows their life, their schedule, their needs, desires, and intentions to interact with the world for them—and with your bot. Yes, get ready to start hearing, "Just have your bot call my bot, and we'll do lunch."

But also get ready for something else—the bad-guy early adopters: "Bots may evolve to be very good at charming people out of their bank account information, persuading them to vote against their interests, or manipulating their emotions." Deep fakes will also hit this industry—fake friends who try to forge fake relationships. "Instead of hacking websites, thieves could hack chatbots to encourage them to perform activities such as requesting people's passwords or social security numbers or sharing bank account information." Therefore, building trust into these systems will become hugely important—and probably the next great industry!

But just don't think it won't be done. "The age of intent is upon us," concludes P.V. "And unless you're preparing for it, you're going to be left behind." So, if I were you, I'd turn the page.

–Thomas L. Friedman

New York Times columnist and
author of *The World Is Flat*

Part I

THE POWER OF INTENT

Chapter 1

"GET ME WHAT I WANT"

In the mid-1990s, a transformation occurred. Prior to the transformation, the main ways that companies interacted with customers were analog: on the phone, in a retail location, or by mail.

But with the advent of the web browser and consumer access to the internet, companies began to create pages of information for customers. Online customers visited those pages and found what they were looking for. Eventually, those pages grew to become sophisticated websites where a customer could find anything she was seeking: answers to support questions; catalogs of products to order from; forms to sign up for things; photos, videos, and ratings.

The web swallowed up the bulk of the interaction between customers and companies because, once it reached maturity, it benefited both the customer and the company.

From the company's perspective, the web was powerful because it created a single set of resources that could be updated at will and delivered automatically on the customer's schedule, vastly reducing the need for staff to answer phone calls and interact in retail locations.

But the web was an improvement in customer experience as well. Customers rapidly learned that if they could find what they were looking for on the web, that experience would be faster, more reliable, and more convenient than dealing with a person working for the company.

Because it was both more efficient for companies and better for customers, the web was transformative. Online interaction has now replaced vast portions of what used to be done by humans. One-eighth of all commerce in the US now goes through digital channels.[1] Whether you are learning, buying, or requesting support, your first stop is the web.

The mobile web has extended this paradigm without fundamentally changing it. Apps make it easier to answer specific questions—"What's my balance?" "Is my flight delayed?"—but cannot replicate the full functionality of the web. The interface remains fundamentally the same.

We have now reached the limits of what is possible with the visual interface of the web. Consider an interaction with your bank, for example. If you want to know your balance, you can use its mobile app. If you want to apply for a credit card, you can do that on your computer screen. But there are hundreds more things you may want to do. You may want to transfer money, cancel a credit card, apply for a home equity loan, or start an investment account. You may want to know why your credit card stopped working, why your check bounced, how much your interest rate is, where your tax documents are, or whether you can increase your credit limit. Many of the answers you are looking for are somewhere on the bank's website. But unless you are very good

at searching—and unless the bank's own content is very easily searchable—you'll probably have trouble finding it. You'll have to fall back on picking up the phone, and the person on the other end of that phone line will have to guide you through solving your problem (or connect you to someone who can).

It's not just banks. When interacting with a retailer, you may want to know which products are in stock, how long one will take to ship, why it didn't arrive on time, or how to return it. At an airline, you may want to know what times flights leave for Cleveland, how long they take to get there, do they require a connection, how much do they cost, what meals are served, what to do if you need to make a change, or whether you can take your schnauzer on board with you. Whether you're dealing with a car company, a telecom company, a theme park, or a real estate broker, the challenge is the same: there are just too many questions and no efficient way to get to the answer.

That's about to change.

A new transformation is now beginning, more than 20 years after the web-driven transformation became mainstream.

In this new world, you will just ask a company to get you what you want, on the phone or using chat. Then the company will go and get it for you—quickly.

The enabling technology for this new kind of interaction is a virtual agent. A virtual agent is a system that uses artificial intelligence to understand what you are looking for and to get it for you.

This is not science fiction. Virtual agents are now helping customers who want to reserve pay-per-view fights on Dish Network, buy business insurance from Allstate, book a room at a Hilton, and ask for help with a flat tire on the car they rented from Avis. Virtual agents are smart—they know what transactions you've already done with the company and what you're likely to want to do next. They're infinitely patient; they don't mind waiting while you track down the expiration date of your car's registration or

the three-digit code on the back of your credit card. And because they can connect with every system inside the company, they can actually complete transactions for you.

Like the web transformation, the virtual agent transformation is better for both the company and the customer.

From the company's perspective, the virtual agent is an efficient machine. Much like the web, it sits and waits for requests, ever ready to answer customers' questions. Like all automated systems, it is designed to be more efficient and less people intensive than current ways of delivering service and information.

But from the customer's perspective, virtual agents are like a miracle. Everyone knows how to ask questions in their natural language. Speaking or chatting with a virtual agent system is easier and more relaxing than searching for information and clicking on links. And there is no longer any need to poke around a website, searching for answers. The virtual agent identifies what you want and gets it for you.

When a technology can actually improve both corporate efficiency *and* customer experience, that technology is going to rapidly make its way through companies. Virtual agents are just now becoming practical, but the results they deliver are dramatic. As they spread, they will forever change the way companies and customers interact.

A different type of interaction

Interactions with websites require the customer to do quite a lot of the work. The basic mode of interaction, from the customer's point of view, looks like this:

Find me what I am seeking, and then I will act on that knowledge.

If the customer is looking for a pair of red pumps and matching handbag, she has to find those pumps and handbag on the site.

The site can help her find them, may even suggest them to her, but it's up to her to seek out what she needs. This is why the most powerful element of web interactions is *search*: it helps you find what you want. Of course, if what you want is to figure out how returns work, or identify what the shipping time and cost will be, or confirm whether the products were sustainably sourced, search might not be the best way to find out. Still, the web is pretty good at delivering what you want—*once you find it.*

With virtual agents, the basic mode of interaction is different. It's much quicker. From the customer's point of view, it looks like this:

Get me what I want.

That's a lot simpler. You just tell the virtual agent, "I want to buy red shoes and a handbag," and it finds them. Or "I want to return the shoes I just got." Or "I want to see what shipping will cost." Or whatever you're seeking.

The challenge, from the company's side, is that it's not so simple to figure out what the customer wants. That's where the artificial intelligence (AI) technology comes in. Computers need to use AI to turn your natural language request (e.g., "I want to return the shoes I just got") into something it can understand. Then it has to match that request to a list of intents—typically one of several hundred for any given industry. (In this case, the name of the intent might be "return product.") And finally, it has to get you to a spot where you can act on the intent.

The new part of this is the identification of intents. But while figuring out the intent is hard, it's a lot easier than, for example, the job of Amazon's Alexa audio assistant. You could ask Amazon's Alexa anything, from the score of the Red Sox game to the text of the Fourteenth Amendment. But if you're interacting with an online shoe store, there are a finite number of possible intents that match up to what the shoe store can do. The same applies to banks, airlines, and telecom companies—each industry has a set of possible intents.

The name of this book is *The Age of Intent* because intent is central to understanding how this transformation works. Understanding the customer's intent—picking it out from what she said—is what makes virtual agents work. Intents are the atomic elements of the virtual agent interaction, just as web pages are the atomic elements of a web interaction.

In this book, I'll show you how the science of intent is making possible a new, more efficient, and more effortless way of interacting between companies and customers. I'll explain what's powering that shift, what it takes for companies to make it, and how it changes their relationships with customers. Finally, I'll explain what the world will look like when anyone can just tell any company, "*Get me what I want.*"

Why this is happening now

When a transformation of this magnitude happens, the timing is crucial. If you are considering investing in this new interaction channel, you need to know just when the fantasy turns to reality, when you can turn the technology into business advantage. Too soon, and you'll waste effort on an immature technology. Too late, and you'll be behind your competitors and unable to catch up.

The moment for virtual agents is now. The reason is that three things are now true:

1. **Intent is knowable.** Computer systems inside companies have a lot of information about you and about the world. Based on knowing who is calling, where you are, what time of day it is, what the weather is, and a lot of other information—*based on context*—a virtual agent can rapidly identify what you are looking for.

2. **Determining intent is possible but difficult.** It's not enough to build simple decision trees that take different decisions based on "if this, then that"-type rules. As anyone who's ever tried to figure out another human being's intent knows, it's easy

to be wrong. Someone needs to teach the system powering the virtual agent about the characteristics of the business and how to model it. Then that system needs massive amounts of data to practice on. After all of this, the system can develop an artificially intelligent algorithm and use it so the virtual agent can make a good guess about what you, the customer, are asking for. Even if that algorithm is effective, it's not static; as business conditions, products, and pricing change, the algorithm powering the virtual agent must also change to keep up.

3. Determining intent is transformative. Like the advent of the web, the advent of AI-powered virtual agents that can figure out what you want will change everything about how companies and their customers interact. A virtual agent that can guess your intent can solve your problem more quickly. It can deliver insights based not just on what customers do but what they *want*. It creates a road map to better customer experiences, which generate loyalty. And it can figure out the exact moment you might be willing to have a deeper relationship, one that is more lucrative to the company.

These are not small, incremental changes. According to *Outside In: The Power of Putting Customers at the Center of Your Business*, the definitive book on customer experience (CX) by Harley Manning and Kerry Bodine, companies that make customer experience improvements see broad and permanent benefits. CX leaders are more likely to see growth, including growth in the value of their stock, than those that lag. But CX improvements are challenging and difficult.

Properly designed virtual agents can improve all customer-facing disciplines, including sales, customer service, and marketing. They can access and act as a front end for the multiple, often poorly integrated, customer systems that exist in every modern company. They're easy for customers to deal with and they reduce the time needed to close a sale or solve a problem. Even when

interacting with an actual person is necessary to solve a problem, virtual agent systems can support them by providing them with the best possible information so they can help customers. Virtual agents represent an inflection point—a rare opportunity to reduce costs and improve customer experience at the same time. The companies that embrace this new way of doing business will develop a significant lead over competitors who haven't yet understood what a difference this new consumer-facing technology will make.

The purpose of this book is to explain the coming of the age of intent, the world where virtual agents at a company can talk to you on the phone, on a website, with a text message, through a smart speaker, or on Facebook; rapidly figure out what you want; and then get it for you with the least hassle. If your company interacts with customers—if customers ever call you or email you—you'll want to know about this. Because it's going to remake your world.

What is it like to talk to a virtual agent that knows what you want?

While the idea of a computer that knows what you want seems amazing, in practice, it results in some pretty straightforward interactions. In contrast to an automated conversation system like Apple's Siri or Amazon's Alexa, a virtual agent is focused only on knowledge that's specific to a given company's customers and their problems.

This makes virtual agents very efficient at getting customers the information they need.

You may have heard these systems referred to as *chatbots*. Chatbots are a broader category that includes not just intelligent personal assistants like Alexa but also any system that provides automated responses to input in the form of voice or text. There are very unsophisticated chatbots—you can easily build one that works on Facebook Messenger, for example. There are very

sophisticated chatbots as well. "Chatbot" is like "web page"—it simply describes a type of interaction between an automated system and a human. What matters is the intelligence and effectiveness of the system behind the chatbot.

Let's look at an example. Suppose you have a SiriusXM Satellite Radio in your car. The radio has stopped working; something is wrong with it. So you go to the SiriusXM website and start chatting by text with a virtual agent—a chatbot—that says it can help. Here's a transcript of just such an interaction that happened recently.

Sirius Chatbot: Hi, I'm the Sirius XM Virtual Agent. I'm here for you.

Sirius Chatbot: How can I help you?

Customer: My radio was not working today, it said I needed to activate it

Sirius Chatbot: Okay, I may be able to help you with that.

Sirius Chatbot: Are you near the radio that's having connection problems?

Customer: I can be

Sirius Chatbot: Awesome! What's the radio ID of the radio that's not working, or the phone number on your account?

[Customer types phone number.]

Sirius Chatbot: Got it. Does your car or radio have a clear view of the sky? Buildings, large trees and garages may interfere with the signal.

Customer: I have to go check

Sirius Chatbot: That could be the problem. Move it to a location with a clear view of the sky and try listening to your channels

Sirius Chatbot: Did that solve the problem?

This seems very simple. But consider that the chatbot on the other end has quite a lot to figure out. It needs to know that "activate" is a word that means the radio needs a signal sent to it—rather than, say, that the customer wants to reset the password or is selling her car. It needs to know that when it asks if the customer is near the radio, a response of "I can be" means neither yes nor no but "wait a minute."

A human could figure these things out . . . but a person would have to look up the subscriber's account and pick out the necessary information. The SiriusXM chatbot knows all that information as well as which kinds of things to suggest based on the customer's responses.

Inside the artificially intelligent system that SiriusXM uses is a list of intents. The list includes such possibilities as cancelling the account due to selling the car, transferring the account to a new car, getting help with credentials and passwords, and sending a signal to reset the radio. The virtual agent that SiriusXM uses, called AIVA, rapidly figured out that the customer needed a signal sent to her radio and walked the customer through all the steps needed to make that happen, including getting the customer's phone number and ensuring that the car wasn't sitting in the garage.

Like all advances in computing that improve the customer's experience, this seems simple, but it isn't. Virtual agents like AIVA are already smarter than human customer service reps in some ways, because they have instant access to all the customer systems and the rest of the context that helps them figure out your intent. They can understand voice as well as text chat. When they get stumped, they can hand the interaction over to a customer service rep along with all the information about what's happened so far and what the customer may be looking for. That means faster, more intelligent service at lower cost.

To understand what that can do for a business, let's take a look at what happened when the car rental company Avis Budget adopted a similar system for its customers in Europe.

How identifying the renter's intent made rentals run smoother for Avis Budget

As travel companies go, Avis Budget has a foot in the future. It owns Zipcar, the company that provides mobile and web-based hourly car rentals for so many millennials. It's working to enable reservations over in-home listening devices like Google Home and Amazon's Alexa Echo. But despite all the technology and the apps, the telephone is still a crucial communications channel for Avis Budget and its customers. After all, when you're driving from Frankfurt to Paris and you realize you need a change in your rental reservation, you're not going to pull over and try to navigate a website. You're going to make a call and hope the rep on the other end of the phone can straighten things out.

A few years back, Avis Budget's chief information officer, Gerard Insall, was pondering the efficiency of the company's North American and European call centers. Two kinds of calls were coming in. The first were nonrevenue calls: requests for changes to reservations, roadside assistance, confirmations, and

cancellations. The second were people actually arranging new reservations. The first type of call cost money; the second made money. Both were crucial for the customer experience of people renting cars. Handle these calls well, and those renters would perceive Avis Budget as a great company to work with; screw up, and they'd just get annoyed and switch rental companies.

A lot of the tedium of calls like that comes from waiting. You interact with an interactive voice response (IVR) system that rattles off six options; inevitably, what you need always seems to be number five or number six. Then you have to dictate your information to a customer service rep. Life would be a lot easier if the company could just figure out what you wanted and confirm it with you.

To accomplish that goal, Insall started working with the executive vice president in charge of the Avis Budget Group call center and with my company, [24]7.ai, to see if we could anticipate what people were calling about.

Right off the bat, it turned out that Avis Budget could identify 35% of callers by matching the phone number of the person calling with the phone numbers that existed in its customer databases. If you called the call center, it could pull up all of your information, including whether you were in the midst of a rental.

If so, the system could make other good guesses as to why you were calling. For example, if you were close to the time you were supposed to return the car, there was a good chance you were trying to extend the rental. If not, the most likely reason was that you needed roadside assistance.

Combine this with improved voice recognition technology, and the interactions with the call center become very different. Instead of navigating a tree of interactive voice response actions and pushing phone buttons, the call might go like this:

[Renter calls number on Avis Budget rental folder from his mobile phone. Avis Budget automated voice answers.]

Avis voice chatbot: Hello, is this Mr. Smith?

Smith: Yes, it is.

Avis: I see you have rented a Volvo from us in Frankfurt on Monday, June 12. Do you need roadside assistance?

Smith: Yes, I have a flat tire.

Avis: We have your location from your mobile phone. Would you like us to send someone out to take care of you?

Smith: Sure, that would be great.

Avis: Please stay on the line. The next voice you hear will be our roadside assistance team.

And after that, the roadside assistance representative would start the conversation already knowing the customer's location. This made arranging the roadside assistance much simpler and faster.

This actually represents one of the more complicated calls. Typical calls involve cancelling reservations, confirming reservations, or getting receipts. The virtual agent on the phone could address all of these issues without involving people at all. Or, in cases where a human representative was eventually needed, the virtual agent could pass along all the necessary information to that representative, thereby making calls far shorter and less annoying.

As I've described, what's different now is that intent is knowable. But understanding that intent isn't simple. The types of

intents that the Avis Budget system understood—intents like "confirm reservation" or "ask for roadside assistance"—came from a comprehensive machine-learning analysis of thousands of calls the call center had handled and interviews with experts and managers in those call centers. Only with their knowledge was it possible to develop ideas about the intents of renters calling in and how to handle those intents.

But once the company implemented the system, knowing the customer's intent created a win-win for both Avis Budget and its customers. From the customer's perspective, it meant less time spent on the phone fighting through "Listen to the following menu" and "Push two to confirm a reservation," leading to a better customer experience. According to Avis Budget's Gerard Insall, the company was able to automate 68% of all the nonrevenue (service) calls, generating savings of millions of dollars a year.

But what about the revenue-generating calls? Making a reservation is a lot more complex than cancelling one. Avis needed a way to make its contact center reps smarter and more efficient while still automating as much as possible. That's where technology made a huge difference.

As Insall explained to me, "We thought it was too complex of a call to automate the whole reservation process. But if we could automate the initial five information elements gathered on every reservation [customer, pickup time, pickup location, drop-off time, drop-off location], if we could perfect that, we could gain back 30 to 45 seconds per call."

Crucially, in contrast to the nonrevenue calls, Insall and his team decided *not* to attempt to automate everything. The number of agents taking these calls would remain the same. They decided to focus instead on the conversion rate—the number of people who completed the reservation.

Sure enough, the new phone system got four or five key pieces of information right 80% of the time, enabling the phone reps to

complete the reservation more quickly and far more often. (As for that other 20%, it's pretty clear that once the technology is in place, it will get smarter, reducing the number of interactions that the system can't immediately figure out.)

Now that the system is in place, Insall has bigger plans. He can implement the exact same system in text chat on the Avis Budget website, or in Facebook Messenger or Apple Business Chat, or in just about any channel that the customer chooses. And since the system knows how to figure out customers' intents—and has confirmed that knowledge over thousands of calls—it's already primed and ready to implement the same efficiencies in the new channels.

Insall can now push forward into new technologies in collaboration with other lines of business at Avis Budget. Successful projects have a way of making changes like that possible.

Time to get your jump on the virtual agent future

What Avis Budget has done, you can do as well. You'd better get started.

If I had told you in 1994 that companies' websites would have a lot to do with their future success, you'd probably have thought I was crazy. But today, a company that doesn't have a well-developed site is far behind. Every industry, from retail to travel to finance, does business through websites.

In 2007, you would have been similarly skeptical if I'd told you that having a mobile app was a crucial element of success. Today everyone needs to have an app or a responsive mobile website; access through mobile is a crucial connection to their customers. Today mobile apps and websites contribute one-third of online sales for retailers.[2]

Soon virtual agents will transform the relationship between your business and your customer, just as the web did 20-plus years

ago. And just as it happened back then, the companies that understand, pilot, learn about, and master the virtual agent transition will gain an advantage over their competitors.

The purpose of this book is to get you ready to seize that advantage. Here's how it's laid out.

Part I: The Power of Intent includes the basics you need to get started with this new technology. In addition to what you just read, it includes a chapter on the clues that a virtual agent system uses to determine not just customers' intent but their frame of mind. I'll also show how data scientists prepare to connect your corpus of data—the historical record of a mass of past interactions with your customers—to train a machine-learning algorithm and how they make all the difference in your virtual agents' effectiveness and improvement over time.

Part II: Applying Intent in Business will give you a look into how companies are actually applying virtual agents in customer-facing situations right now. In three successive chapters, you'll see how the Swedish bank SEB improved customer service with virtual agents, how TGI Fridays generated huge gains in business from a Facebook chatbot, and how InterContinental Hotel Group is using chatbots to help employees be more productive.

Part III: Succeeding with Virtual Agents goes into more detail on what it takes to make a virtual agent system successful under actual business conditions. In this section, you'll see how to approach powerful conversational platform channels like Facebook Messenger and Amazon Alexa, how to win over your own management teams, how to upgrade your information architecture to work with virtual agents, and how to analyze your customers' journeys to optimize your virtual agent system.

Part IV: The Virtual Agent Future is a complete road map of the future transformation from our current ways of interacting to the age of intent—what it means for your staffing, your strategy, and your company's position in the world.

Glossary

Here's a quick set of definitions in case you need to refer back to them later in the book:

- **Application program interface (API)**—A set of protocols that allow computer systems to communicate and share data with each other. For example, an API could allow a virtual agent system to query a banking system about a specific customer's bank balance.

- **Artificial intelligence (AI)**—Any type of computing in which a computer simulates processes typically done by humans. AI includes machine learning and natural language processing.

- **Bot**—Short for chatbot.

- **Chatbot**—Any automated system that a human can converse with by voice or by text chat. Virtual agents are one class of chatbot.

- **Containment**—A term for calls or chats where the virtual agent can solve the problem on its own, without referring the question to a human agent. The percentage of calls or chats handled solely by the virtual agent is the *containment rate.*

- **Corpus**—A body of data, such as the complete transcripts of all the text chats that human support reps have had with customers, along with other data attributes about those conversations.

- **Conversational commerce**—Using virtual agents and chatbots to complete sales. For more detail, see chapter 7.

- **Conversational computing**—A general term that encompasses all interactions in which humans converse with automated systems, such as virtual agents, chatbots, and intelligent assistants.

- **Conversational platform**—A conversational system created and managed by a technology company in which people can converse with chatbots. Examples include Facebook Messenger (for text chat) and Amazon Alexa (for voice interactions). For more detail, see chapter 6.

- **Customer experience (CX)**—The sum total of all experiences that a customer has with a company; the business discipline of analyzing such experiences. Research shows that improving customer experience leads to growth and profit.

- **Customer journey**—The path a customer takes to accomplish a goal.

- **Customer journey analytics (CJA)**—The science of applying data to get insights about customer journeys across all channels and all customers. For more detail, see chapter 9.

- **Intelligent assistant**—A system designed to answer general questions posed to it by voice. Notable examples are Amazon's Alexa, Apple's Siri, Google Assistant, and Microsoft Cortana. While intelligent assistants answer

general questions, virtual agents answer questions specific to a company, such as customer service questions.

- **Intent**—In the context of a virtual agent system, intent is a determination of what a customer wants from an interaction with a company, picked out from a finite list of possible intents. Examples could include "return a product" or "cancel a credit card."
- **Interactive voice response (IVR)**—A telephone system that customers interact with and navigate, typically by pressing phone buttons. Think "Press one for customer service, two for customer support . . ."
- **Machine learning**—A discipline of AI in which computerized systems analyze a corpus of data and identify patterns, which can then be used to predict intents and model responses.
- **Natural language processing**—A discipline of AI that allows computers to derive meaning from speech or written language.
- **Path bound**—Describes a bot that follows a specific "if-then" sequence of questions and answers, as opposed to interpreting the user's questions through AI.
- **Robotic process automation (RPA)**—A mechanism that allows computers or people to quickly perform a set of actions that would normally require typing and clicking on an interface, such as setting up a shipping form or registering a new customer.

- **Smart speaker**—A device that allows a human to talk to an intelligent assistant, such as Amazon's Alexa Echo or the Google Home Mini.

- **Systems of engagement**—Corporate computer systems built close to the channels where customers interact, such as mobile apps and websites. For more detail, see chapter 8.

- **Systems of intelligence**—Systems that span and connect the systems of record with the systems of engagement.

- **Systems of record**—The base systems that manage the data that a company runs on, such as customer databases, reservations systems, and product information systems.

- **Technical debt**—The accumulation of problems due to failing to invest in keeping corporate systems up to date.

- **Virtual agent**—An artificially intelligent system that a human can converse with by voice or by text chat. Virtual agents use all possible context to determine how to interpret and respond to questions from customers or employees.

Chapter 2

INTENT IS FUNDAMENTAL

Matias Fras is a very efficient man. He knows that technology creates opportunity, but seizing that opportunity takes work. He spent 12 years at Accenture helping European companies across a variety of industries—from steel to media to health care—to hone their strategies in a changing world.

So as he began working at Nordea, the largest bank in the Nordic countries and one of the 40 largest banks in the world, it became natural to focus on efficiency—and particularly on the efficiencies that AI could deliver.

Some of Fras's first efforts focused on robotic process automation (RPA). In RPA, the company identifies a series of actions that are typically taken by human workers across multiple banking systems and then creates a piece of software to do the same thing. (I describe RPA in more detail in chapter 5.)

RPA started to make improvements in processes in the fall of 2016. And it was a success at Nordea, making many processes faster and more efficient. By August of 2018, Nordea had deployed about 250 RPA bots completing about a quarter of a million tasks every month.

After that, Fras naturally asked the question: Could we bring the same approach to helping customers?

This was the genesis of the project called "Nova." Nova was to be a chatbot that would read customers' questions from a chat window, interpret them, and then seek out the answers. Part of the impetus for Nova was that many of the answers people sought were already present on the bank's website, but not in a way that was easy to find. Bank customers approaching the site might have any of 1,500 different banking intents. Unless Nova could identify those intents and connect customers to the right information, it would be less efficient than a customer service representative answering the telephone.

Nova came into existence as a result of an intense effort over the first half of 2017. A task force of between five and ten staffers worked on it for five months. Most of that effort was spent preparing the internal banking systems to respond appropriately to requests from a virtual agent.

Nova went live in mid-2017, and when it rolled out, it was a big success. It could identify consumers' intents in 87% of cases.

Nova wasn't designed to work like a machine; it was designed to respond as a person would. "We want Nova to be warm, expert, and kind. These are the values that she should convey," Fras says. "We made sure all the answers she gives are aligned with those values and principles." A virtual agent should institutionalize the values your company aspires to.

Customers have responded positively. According to Fras, once the company put Nova in place, it reduced emails and calls by 25% almost immediately. It also increased traffic to web pages with

relevant answers by 33%. People were finding what they were looking for. And Fras has evidence that customers like it better.

As Fras explained to me, "It's not about a new channel toward the customer. It's about reimagining the customer experience." He expects that tools like Nova will slowly but fundamentally change the way a person interacts with the bank. "You will not do mobile banking, phone, or email," he predicts. "Nova will provide you with recommendations, savings advice, pretty much anything that people in the branches or on the phone could do: full service. This is a revolution from the customer perspective."

That level of success is continuing to increase as the people who are building Nova identify more cases that it's missing and add appropriate responses. Nova has grown to the point where it now handles 20,000 conversations per month and is available not just on the Nordea site but also on its mobile app.

Consider, for a moment, the significance of what Nordea has done. It has improved customer experience and made customers happier. Customers like a tool that gets them reliable answers more quickly. Behind that experience is an artificial intelligence. Within that artificial intelligence is an efficient engine that can read the language in a chat window and pick out one of 1,500 separate possible customer intents, from opening a business account to expanding a credit limit to reporting a fraudulent charge.

Intent is the key to the revolution that Matias Fras is bringing to banking—and it's the fundamental concept behind every virtual agent transformation.

What is intent?

Intent is fundamental to the coming changes in customer experience. But it's also a remarkably subtle concept. Let's spend a little time on the question of what intent truly means in the context of a virtual agent system. Here's the relevant definition:

Intent is a determination of what a customer wants from an interaction with a company.

As I described in chapter 1, the intent is the fundamental unit of interaction for a virtual agent system. In the web era, the customer said, "Find me what I am seeking," and ended up on a page that had it. In the age of intent, the customer says, "Get me what I want," and the virtual agents goes and gets it. The "what I want" is the intent.

To be manageable, the list of intents for any company must be relatively small: in the hundreds, or possibly in the thousands, but not in the hundreds of thousands. So any system that deals with intents must do so at the right level of granularity. "Fix the problem in my account" is too general; it is not a desire that any human or virtual agent could respond to because it's fuzzy. "Delete the spurious charge of $127.50 for the track shoes I never bought" is too specific; it's certainly a desire, but customers at any company might have millions of different desires at this level of detail. "I want to delete a charge from my card" is the right level of detail for an intent that a virtual agent can act on.

Once a virtual agent has identified an intent like this, it typically follows a clear series of steps regarding what to do next (for example, get the customer to identify the charge, verify that it is an error, process a credit for it). Even if the customer has a specific desire, the set of steps to deal with that desire starts at the level of the more general intent.

The key to unlocking intents at this level is to recognize that similar businesses will have similar sets of intents. For example, in a retail business, a customer might want to find a product, buy a product, determine shipping costs, find a store close by, or return a product. In a telecom business, a customer might want to start service, upgrade, solve a technical problem, or dispute a charge on a bill. Because all retail businesses and all telecom businesses have similar sets of intents, this creates efficiencies.

When a vendor like [24]7.ai creates a recognition algorithm that can identify intent from a list of intents for one company—say, a retailer—it can apply that same recognition algorithm to many other similar types of businesses (in this case, other retailers).

For example, here's an abridged list of common intents in retail.

CATEGORY	DESCRIPTION
Account	Delete customer account
Account	Change account information
Account	Setup a new account
Account	Reset password for an account
Marketing	Complaint about wrong or inaccurate information on website
Marketing	Opt out of marketing mailing lists
Marketing	Question about current promotions or discounts
Store	Find a store
Product	Get information about a product
Product	Get information about parts or accessories for the product
Product	Get information about the supplier or manufacturer of a product
Product	Check online availability of the product (or expected availability if currently out of stock)
Product	Check in-store availability of the product (or expected availability if currently out of stock)
Product	Check availability for ordering item online and picking it up in-store
Product	Check for upgrade eligibility and request upgrade (e.g., phone and plan)
Product	Get details of current service plan
Product	Get details of existing contract (e.g., phone contract), such as payments and expiration date

CATEGORY	DESCRIPTION
Order	Question or concern about item price
Order	Request price match with another retailer
Order	Request price match between website and in-store
Order	Get help with placing an order online
Order	Request backorder for an item that is not available or not in stock
Order	Problem placing an order
Order	Apply discount or promotion
Order	Apply employee discount
Order	Request gift wrapping
Order	Issue with order total at checkout
Shipping	Get shipping options and costs
Shipping	Request expedited shipping
Shipping	Apply shipping promotion
Shipping	Request waiver of shipping charges
Shipping	Problem with entering the shipping address
Shipping	Ship to store or pick up item in store
Delivery	Order not received
Delivery	Order received but one or more items are missing or incomplete
Delivery	Item received does not match the item ordered
Delivery	Item received is damaged
Delivery	Item received is defective
Delivery	Item received does not fit or is not appropriate for its intended purpose
Delivery	Packing slip missing from shipment
Delivery	Item received but card was not charged
Return	Return an item and receive a refund
Return	Check the status of a return or refund

CATEGORY	DESCRIPTION
Return	Check if an item can be returned to store
Return	Request a replacement order
Return	Request a return label
TechSupport	Schedule a technician visit
TechSupport	Reschedule a technician visit
TechSupport	Cancel a technician visit
TechSupport	Confirm or get details of a technician visit
TechSupport	Get ETA of a technician visit

And here's an abridged list of some intents for the telecom business. Notice how many of these intents are different from those in the list for retailers. That's because a person looking for help from a telecom company has needs that are different from the needs of a person contacting a retailer.

CATEGORY	DESCRIPTION
Account	Get information on an existing account (e.g., address, email ID, etc.)
Account	Delete customer account
Account	Change account information (e.g., contact details, password)
Account	Setup or register a new account
Account	Problems registering a new account
Marketing	Opt out of marketing mailing lists
Corporate	Get the phone number for Customer Care or other department
Corporate	Problems accessing the website
Corporate	Turn off cookies
Store	Find a store

CATEGORY	DESCRIPTION
Store	Get information about a store
Plan	Check if a product (TV, internet, fixed line) is available at a specific address
Plan	Information on product bundles
Plan	Get details of current contract and plan
Plan	Change a plan or package (upgrade or downgrade)
Plan	Cancel an existing plan
Plan	Information or assistance with signing up for a trial plan
Mobile	Change a mobile plan (upgrade or downgrade)
Mobile	Cancel a mobile plan
Mobile	Add a line to a mobile plan
Mobile	Purchase a SIM card and order a plan for a phone or mobile device
Mobile	Purchase a mobile broadband device and plan (USB modems, tablets, etc.)
Mobile	Set up mobile services, such as voicemail
HomePhone	Information or assistance with ordering a fixed phone line
HomePhone	Change a home phone plan
HomePhone	Cancel a home phone plan
HomePhone	Add a line to a fixed phone plan
HomePhone	Purchase a home phone outright
TV	Information or assistance with ordering a TV plan
TV	Change a TV plan (upgrade or downgrade)
TV	Cancel a TV plan
TV	Question on TV outage
TV	Set up a device

Lists like these give the virtual agent a limited selection of possible intents to choose from. In the terminology of customer experience experts, these intents define elements of customer journeys—paths that customers travel to accomplish their goals. In fact, as I'll describe in chapter 9, there is an entire science dedicated to analyzing how customers on these journeys get to appropriate and predictable resolutions: customer journey analytics.

But even with a list of intents like this, determining a customer's exact intent is remarkably subtle. Remember, the virtual agent starts only with the text that a customer types or with what a voice says on the phone. Different words can mean different things in different contexts.

Don't believe me? Consider, for a moment, having a conversation with your spouse, who says this: "I've had a very hard day. My boss was completely unreasonable today. I've had it with that guy."

What is your spouse's intent?

Do you think your spouse's intent is to get help with solving a problem with their boss? If so, then your response should be to learn more about the situation and help your spouse think through solving the problem.

Or is your spouse just really upset? Maybe they're venting, and their intent is just to get some sympathy. If so, you should say something like "Wow, dear, that sounds terrible," and then just listen for a while.

Anyone who's ever been in a relationship knows that it is perilous to mistake one of these intents for the other. And yet both intents get introduced with the very same words.

This is why contextual elements are important. This includes emotional context (is the spouse concentrating or looking furious?), past history (how many times have you heard this complaint this month?), and what you've learned in the past (did they shout, "You just don't get it!" and slam the door when you tried the logical problem-solving approach?).

The smart move is to take all this contextual knowledge into account and, possibly, to ask something like, "Do you want me to help you with the problem, or are you just venting frustration?"

In the same way, the virtual agent must take into account not just the words that are coming from the customer but the customer's past history and other types of context to make a decision. And like you, the virtual agent may need to ask a question or two to clarify the intent.

No simple set of "if this, then that"-type statements is sufficient to identify intent from all the available information. But determining intent is not beyond the capability of a computer. What it takes is a system that can anticipate, simplify, and then learn—with the aid of artificial intelligence.

How AI works in virtual agents: Anticipate, simplify, learn

Articles about artificial intelligence tend to describe it as if it were something magical. For decades, the term "artificial intelligence" referred to technologies that were perpetually in the future. This is because of what is known as the "AI effect." As Pamela McCorduck wrote in her book *Machines Who Think*, "It's part of the history of the field of artificial intelligence that every time somebody figured out how to make a computer do something—play good checkers, solve simple but relatively informal problems—there was a chorus of critics to say 'that's not thinking.'"

In the same sense, creating a virtual agent that can answer a customer's question seems magical—until you explain how it works. Yes, this explanation uses techniques traditionally described by the term "artificial intelligence," such as machine learning. It's not something your whiz-kid programmer can whip up in her lab in a couple of days—yet. But I'll try to take the concept apart for you so you can understand the steps, all of

which are based on the fundamental concept of intent.

To understand how a virtual agent system works, think about three steps:

1. Anticipate—train a virtual agent to identify intent.

2. Simplify—design that system to effectively act on each intent.

3. Learn—improve the system so that it can handle a greater variety of intents more effectively.

Anticipate: Training a virtual agent to identify intent

Imagine for a moment that you are a weather forecaster in Boston, Massachusetts. A low-pressure system is coming in from the west. What will happen next?

Well, that depends.

What is the temperature?

What is the jet stream doing?

What other weather systems are in the area?

To make a smart prediction, you would look at thousands of past situations that were something like this one. You would see if you could determine which elements of the situation would best predict the outcome. Then you would build a model based on those elements that would tell you whether to predict a light drizzle, coastal flooding, or sunshine two days later.

If you build the model properly, it will enable you to *anticipate* any weather situation. You just look at what's happening and enter the information, and the model tells you what to expect based on similar past situations.

This is, basically, what happens with virtual agents.

A company is receiving thousands of support calls and chats. To train the virtual agent, the company and its data scientists must create what's called a *corpus of data* from the transcripts of those calls and chats. Each record in the corpus is a single call or chat (in our analogy, that would correspond to a single set of weather readings). The record includes the words that the customer used as well as the words that the support representative used in response. There are contextual variables too: was the customer's account overdrawn, was her plane late, is this a very loyal customer or a new customer, did she just complete a transaction, and so on. The intent is analogous to the actual weather outcome in our analogy—it represents the right "answer" to this particular situation.

Computers that can see the outcomes of those calls and chats can help with adding these intents to the records. For example, if the support representative completes the call by increasing someone's credit limit, it makes sense to identify "increase credit limit" as the customer's intent.

This corpus of data then becomes the training data for the machine-learning algorithm, which looks for patterns in the data.

Weather predictions a few days out may or may not be accurate. But in the case of a virtual agent, you'd like to be able to identify the intent with a high degree of accuracy. (You don't want to be a problem solver when the customer just wants to vent, for example, or vice versa.)

That means the corpus of training data may include thousands of possible input variables. Mathematically, the prediction algorithm then determines how any of those variables contribute to the probability of any given intent. This is a technique often used in natural language processing for performing statistical analysis of texts, a variant of the method called multiple regression. The prediction algorithm looks at the presence or absence of each individual word, each pair of words (digram), and each triplet of

words (trigram) in the chat. It also looks at all the other variables, such as whether the account is overdrawn or the customer has just placed an order.

Training the virtual agent on all this data might take days of processing time. But at the end of all that crunching and analysis, the virtual agent model can calculate which words and contexts in a chat are most likely to correlate with each intent.

So just as a weather model might tell you to anticipate two inches of rain and 50-mile-per-hour winds in a couple of days, the virtual agent system, trained on data from actual customers, can anticipate customers' intents based on what they say (or type). At Nordea, the system gets the intent right 87% of the time.

There's a twist here, and it comes from emotion. Remember when I described the challenge of knowing if your spouse wanted help with a problem or wanted sympathy? In the same way, the virtual agent system may need to identify the customer's emotional state. For example, words like "I could use your help" could indicate a patient customer, while profanity might indicate one who is impatient. The emotional state, along with the other variables, could help determine the ideal response in any given interaction.

Simplify: Design that system to effectively act on each intent

What does the virtual agent do once it has identified the intent? It does whatever a human agent would do.

The identification is the hard part. A human agent knows, for example, that if there is a spurious charge on a credit card, the agent must temporarily remove it and then start a process to verify that it is indeed false. Or if the customer wants to order a product that is out of stock, the virtual agent must suggest substitutes or create an alert that will tell the customer when it is available again.

Typically, *identifying* problems is much harder than *solving*

those problems once identified. In the simplify phase, you design the system to solve the problems based on the customers' intents.

Let's look at some examples.

Here are a couple of actual interactions with a chatbot from a major hotel chain. (You can see typos and unconventional capitalization in these examples because that's how people actually interact with virtual agents; they aren't perfect typists.)

Chatbot: Hello, I am [hotel chain's] Virtual Assistant and can help with some of your questions. If I don't have an answer, I'll pass you to a live agent. How can I help?

Customer: Hello!

Chatbot: Hello, how can I help you?

Customer: good afternoon! I will be in this hotel between November 30 and December 2 and then between Dec 9 and December 13 ([name of hotel]). I did some Amazon shopping that should be delivered to the hotel. please, in case the packages arrive at the hotel before my arrival, save them for me.

Chatbot: Most [of our] properties will hold packages for guests. Please make sure the package label is addressed to the hotel and includes the guest's name, arrival date, and reservation confirmation number. Please note that our properties will not accept packages that are sent C.O.D. (Cash on delivery).

Chatbot: Was the response helpful?

Customer: Yes

Customer: Tks!

In this case, the chatbot has correctly identified the intent—the customer wants to get packages delivered to hotel—and responded with the exact information intended to solve the customer's problem.

Here's another interaction from the same hotel chatbot.

Chatbot: Hello, I am [hotel chain's] Virtual Assistant and can help with some of your questions. If I don't have an answer, I'll pass you to a live agent. How can I help?

Customer: need to cancel and seek refund for my reservation due to severe winter storm advisory for the Chicago area.

Chatbot: Do you have a confirmed reservation?

Customer: Yes

Chatbot: To determine if your reservation is eligible for cancellation please review your cancellation policy for your stay. For confirmed reservations your cancellation policy can be found in the following locations:
-Your reservation confirmation e-mail
-When logged in to your account, and looking at stay details it can be found in the rules & restrictions section. Click "View/Edit" next to the reservation you'd like to cancel. Then, click "Cancel this reservation" to complete your cancellation.

Chatbot: Was the response helpful?

Customer: Yes

In this case, there's a bit more dialogue because the chatbot must first determine that the intent is to cancel the reservation,

then ask if it is confirmed, and finally point the customer to the correct information in the reservation confirmation email or in the customer's online account. Unlike the SiriusXM chatbot in the previous chapter, this chatbot does not attempt to authenticate the specific customer and check her individual reservation; instead, the chatbot tells the customer how to check this information herself. Actually determining the details of this reservation would require authenticating who the customer is, which is possible but a little more complicated, as I describe in chapter 8.

Sometimes solving the problem requires an extended dialogue and walking the customer through a multistep process. For example, here's a transcript from Dish Network, the satellite television operator. DiVA is the name of the virtual agent system.

Dish Virtual Agent: Hi, I'm the Dish virtual agent. I can help you with many things. If I can't, I'll connect you with someone who can. How can I help you?

Customer: My remote has stopped working with my tv but still lights up

DiVA: As a virtual agent, I am programmed to learn from my mistakes. Rephrase what you just wrote and if I don't get it right this time, I'll connect you with someone who can assist you. How can I help you?

Customer: My remote isn't connected to my tv anymore

At this point, the virtual agent is able to identify the intent, which is to set up the TV remote. What happens next is a simple series of steps, which the infinitely patient virtual agent is able to walk the customer through.

DiVA: Before we begin, does your remote have a clear line of sight to the TV and receiver? Objects between the remote and TV or receiver may cause the signal to be blocked.

Customer: Yes

DiVA: Are the batteries in the remote fresh?

Customer: Yes

DiVA: Okay, let's identify your remote. Look on the back for a 3-digit number. It's either near the top or engraved on the battery cover. Select the button below that matches that number.

Customer: 54.0

DiVA: Step 1 of 10: Press HOME twice on your remote. When you're done with that, select Next.

Customer: Next

DiVA: Do you see this screen?

[Shows graphic of TV screen]

Customer: Yes

DiVA: Step 2 of 10: Good, now select Settings on your TV.

Customer: Next

DiVA: Step 3 of 10: Select Remote Control.

Customer: Next

DiVA: Step 4 of 10: Arrow to and select TV.

Customer: Next

[Continues for 4 more steps . . .]

DiVA: Step 8 of 10: Press VOLUME UP to test the remote.

Customer: Next

DiVA: Step 9 of 10: Did the TV volume get louder?

Customer: Yes

DiVA: Step 10 of 10: Great! Now arrow to and select Finished and you're all set. Was this helpful?

Customer: Yes

DiVA: Is there anything else I can do for you today?

Customer: No

DiVA: Thank you for being a valued Dish customer. Have a great day!

To recap, the part that requires artificial intelligence and machine learning is anticipating what the customer wants—identifying the intent. After that, it's a simple matter to create a

set of steps for each intent to solve the customer's problem. (I'll review more of how Dish Network began to implement virtual agents in the next chapter.)

What happens when the system can't identify the intent? That's where the third step, "learn," comes in.

Learn: Improve the system so that it can handle a greater variety of intents more effectively

All virtual agent systems have holes in them. Sometimes, they guess the wrong intent. Sometimes, they can't figure out the intent at all.

This is not a failure. Even if the virtual agent can't figure out the intent half the time, it's still going to make the whole system more efficient. Half the time, customers will quickly and consistently get what they're looking for. The other half, they'll quickly get handed over to a human agent who can solve the problem in the usual way.

But virtual agent systems aren't static. They can improve.

When the virtual agent has been in place for a while, the company can generate a new corpus of data from its failures—the places where it got an intent wrong or couldn't figure things out. With this new corpus, the data scientists can train the system to be more accurate. With a little help from its handlers, the machine literally learns from its mistakes.

This is what Matias Fras from Nordea means when he says that his virtual agent Nova's 87% accuracy in identifying intents was improving. His AI trainers are continually helping it to identify the intents it had missed. He emphasizes that AI isn't static—it improves because of his staff's continuing efforts.

Learning is also necessary because the world changes. Companies introduce new products. Customers develop new needs. A question like "Can I stream video content?" would have

been unheard of for Dish Network in 2010, but in 2019, it's a natural question.

But learning new intents—and becoming more accurate at identifying them—is a lot easier for a machine than for people. In the case of human agents, these updates require training a whole bunch of people. In the case of a virtual agent, it only needs to improve once, and it can help a whole new set of customers.

Intents are building blocks: What you build with them is up to you

I said that in the age of intent, the intents are the atomic elements—just as web pages were the building blocks of the web era.

If I had explained web pages to you in 1994, you might have guessed that they would redefine the relationship between companies and customers. But would you have realized that you could build Amazon.com out of them? Or CNN.com? Or E-Trade?

In the same way, the building blocks of intent are poised to once again redefine the relationship between companies and customers. But the actual impact of that transformation will ripple through industries and departments in more ways than we can imagine.

Already, though, intent is redefining relationships in three disciplines: customer service, sales, and employee communication. I'll show how intents and virtual agents will transform these disciplines in the next three chapters.

Part II

APPLYING INTENT IN BUSINESS

Chapter 3

VIRTUAL AGENTS TRANSFORM CUSTOMER SERVICE

Lucky Rai was a Dish Network customer long before he started to work there. His first exposure to the satellite TV service was as a child in a first-generation family of immigrants—a family for whom Dish Network's dozens of authentic Indian channels were an essential part of the family's home entertainment.

So in 2011, when he took his MBA and customer experience training and started looking for a job in Denver, Dish Network looked like a good place to land. By 2017, he'd been promoted six times and had risen to a director-level position in customer service. He'd also realized that for Dish to keep succeeding, it had to solve customer pain points quickly, easily, and efficiently.

In contrast to cable TV, where customer service challenges are a constant problem, satellite TV has a much better service

reputation. But all pay TV customers are impatient. People want what they want and they want it now, whether that means fixing a channel lineup, untangling confusion about a bill, setting up a new TV set, or signing up to see a pay-per-view fight. Customer service agents delivering on that expectation—whether by phone or through online chat—face challenges because they might have to check seven different customer systems to look up information and guide the customer through the required steps.

Lucky knew that the shortest path to improving that experience had to be digital. Among the digital technologies he investigated, virtual agents looked promising because they answered common questions with infinite patience. Lucky eventually asked my colleagues and me to build him a virtual agent system called DiVA (Dish Interactive Virtual Agent).

When you read press reports about robots, you see story after story about how they are coming to take our jobs. And when you read articles about customer service changes, they always seem to be about saving money by doing things more cheaply. Put those two common stories together, and you might imagine that the point of DiVA was to save money by automating customer service.

But that was never the plan at Dish Network.

As Lucky told me, "The simple 'Replace people with bots' idea is not practical. There is no replacement for interactions with an agent. The level of empathy is not there. But what we *can* do is eliminate the simple pain points. Virtual agents allow us to better understand intent, to serve the customer with an experience that can complement it.

"Our company's mission is to transcend our industry in customer experience, not just to focus on operational expenses," he explains. Dish Network already delivers the best customer service among pay TV providers in the US, according to J. D. Power.[1] Lucky and his team at Dish were determined to maintain and improve that service.

As I write this, Dish has less than a year of experience with customers interacting with DiVA. But the results are encouraging.

Dish started by automating the most common 30% of customers' intents, answering a set of questions that account for about 4 million customer interactions per year. As a result, you can now use chat with the virtual agent to ask a simple question like, "What channel is the Super Bowl on?" But it can also walk you through more complex interactions, such as how to get your TV set to work with the Dish Network remote as we described in the previous chapter. It will even help you get an extension on your bill if your finances are a bit tight this month.

Across that first set of intents, DiVA now handles 40% of customers' questions on its own, without involving any human support agents. Satisfaction levels are comparable to answers from Dish customer support reps. In many cases, Lucky says, people report that they enjoy interacting with DiVA. But more importantly, Dish has taken a significant step toward moving customers' service questions into a digital communications channel and integrating them with the rest of its digital operation.

This has generated several key advantages that actually improve the level of service Dish can offer.

First, DiVA chat is available all day and all night. Human agents, not surprisingly, aren't. If you need help at two in the morning, DiVA can help you.

Second, DiVA quickly connects with legacy customer information systems at Dish, so it can rapidly answer questions like, "When is my bill due?" or "Is this channel in the package I signed up for?"

Third, it's patient in a way that human agents can't be. Maybe you're a whiz at hooking up electronics. But if you're not, and you know it's going to take you thirty minutes to carefully go through the steps to set up your TV to work with your Dish remote, DiVA will patiently wait for you to complete each step. While it's talking to you, it can be talking to hundreds or thousands of

other customers at the same time, with no perceptible lag in its response time. Virtual agent systems scale in a way that entirely human contact centers simply cannot.

The ongoing shift at Dish is causing the satellite operator to rethink how it measures the success of customer service—and how to improve it.

"We used to associate call rate with customer experience," Lucky says. "When fewer customers called, we thought we were doing a good job. But when we took a step back, we realized that our customers may not be calling us as much as they used to because of digital channels. They interact with our apps and with our set-top boxes. The total number of interactions might be the same, even if the call-in rate is dropping year over year."

"Handle time," a typical customer service metric, is no longer a clear measure of customer service effectiveness. When human agents are handling calls or text chats and handle time goes up, that could indicate a problem (and tax capacity at the contact center). But when a virtual agent's handle time goes up, that could just indicate that the customer needed more help and wanted to go at a more deliberate pace. Taking longer is no longer necessarily a problem.

With DiVA in place, Dish can continue to improve customer service in multiple directions.

Lucky's team has already moved the level of satisfaction with DiVA chats from 50% to close to 70%, simply by rewriting the virtual agents' scripts to be more genuine and empathetic.

Dish is planning to double the number of intents that DiVA can handle by connecting it with transactional systems, such as the system that allows a customer to sign up for HBO or upgrade her television package.

And Dish will figure out what it takes to get the "containment rate"—the percent of DiVA calls that don't end up being referred to a human agent—above the current 40%. That will improve, in

part, as customers get more comfortable chatting with machines. Conversational systems like Amazon's Alexa and Apple's Siri will help with those attitudes.

Dish is now exploring moving DiVA into its telephone support channel, where the virtual agent system will understand and answer telephone calls as well as chats.

And what of the contact center agents? They're actually happier; they've been freed of the more routine customer requests, so they can apply their skills to the ones that are more complex or require a bit more care and empathy. Even when DiVA kicks a chat out to an agent, it continues running in the background, where it shares with the agent what already happened, what it believes the customer's problem is, and what might be the best way to help her.

The next generation of customer service at Dish—and at every customer service operation—is a hybrid future that includes both human and virtual agents working together to handle the load. That's a future where service will become more and more digital as people like Lucky figure out the best ways to blend the capabilities of human empathy and AI-driven customer service.

A new day for customer service

Customer service has been squeezed between costs and quality for decades. In the '90s, companies switched to interactive voice response (IVR) systems that required customers to navigate voice menus. In the early 2000s, telephone service moved offshore, with representatives in call centers in places like India and the Philippines. Then came online chat, which allowed reps to handle two, three, or even more conversations at the same time.

Each of those changes reduced costs. But each also created new challenges for the customers navigating the system. While costs per contact have come down, customer satisfaction remains

stagnant. The aggregate customer satisfaction index of the American Customer Satisfaction Index (ACSI), which measures customer satisfaction scores, has bounced around from 74 in 1995 to 76.7 in 2017 and has never reached above 77.[2] And according to Dimension Data, customer satisfaction scores decreased by 10 percentage points in 2017, from 78% to 68%.[3]

This squeeze was inevitable so long as companies saw customer service as a cost center. But a new realization is sweeping across the customer service industry.

Customer service is central to customer experience. And customer experience drives loyalty and profits.

Consider banks, where direct deposit, ATMs, debit cards, and mobile check deposits mean you hardly ever need to come into a branch anymore. Or mobile telecom services, where you can buy your phone from an online store, connect it, set up your service, and pay your bill online, never even speaking with a person. Or Dish Network, where once the satellite dish is set up, you never need to see the service staff again.

With these sorts of twenty-first-century relationships, the customer service interaction is no longer a cost center. Instead, it's one of the few instances where the company has the ability to delight customers and exceed expectations. In a world like that, saving a few pennies on a support call is far less important than getting the interaction right and making the consumer happy.

As customer service guru Frank Eliason, author of the book *@Your Service*, says, "Your call center is not a cost center, but instead it is the hub for the ongoing, fruitful relationship with your customer."

Ease of migration means that consumers are no longer locked into services. In telecom, for example, T-Mobile demolished long-term contracts and wooed customers away from other mobile providers. Millennials might go into a shoe store one day and find the perfect pair of athletic shoes, then buy the same thing from

Zappos six months later, and every six months after that. If you get sick of your TV service, Dish Network, DirecTV, or your local cable operator would be happy to set you up with them, or you might get impatient enough to cut the cord and stream everything.

Mike Pace, renowned customer service expert and president of the Northeast Contact Center Forum, explained it to me simply: "It's incredibly easy to have customers come and go. And churn [customers defecting to competitors] can be the death of a company."

Customer service is a customer reaching out to have a conversation. It's an opportunity to shine.

And these days, the more effective you are with digital tools, the brighter you'll shine in that interaction.

Seven ways that virtual agents improve customer service

Once you recognize that virtual agents aren't primarily about squeezing out costs, you can see the big picture: how they position your service operation to generate a better experience, build loyalty, and focus humans on what humans do best, which is to solve complicated problems and make emotional connections.

In reviewing the experience of many companies deploying virtual agents, I've identified seven ways in which they make the customer experience better. Virtual agents improve:

1. Consistency—give the same right answer every time.

2. Uptime—make service available 24/7.

3. Capacity—scale up to serve customers quickly, even during peak service periods.

4. Speed—reduce time spent waiting for human agents.

5. Productivity—help human agents deliver smarter and better service.

6. Intelligence—generate new insights by analyzing aggregated service interactions.

7. Channel independence—consumers can use voice or text chat and get the same answers from the same bot.

Virtual agents help manage the challenge of consistency

If you're not a customer service professional, you may have no idea just how hard it is to ensure that customer service agents give a consistent set of answers to common questions.

According to service expert Mike Pace, it's commonplace for agents to be looking at between six and 20 different applications on dual monitors as they attempt to solve your problem. Those applications might include customer databases, pricing matrices, policy manuals, billing systems, knowledge bases of problems and solutions, and so on. Integrating those systems into a "single view of the customer" is a very nice dream to have, but in the real world, those system integrations are costly and never seem to reach completion. The systems are effectively integrated in one place: in the mind of the agent, who is attempting to pull all the information together and apply it to solving this customer's problem at this moment.

Chat systems have added to the agent's challenge. In many cases, chat agents are handling two or more inquiries at once, which increases their cognitive load and the challenges they must manage to give a consistent answer every single time.

As Forrester Research analyst Kate Leggett explains in her

report *Transform the Contact Center for Customer Service Excellence*, "This lack of a standardized discovery process—and failure to automate wherever and whenever possible—hinders agent consistency and productivity, lengthens agent training times, and increases agent turnover due to frustration with the tool set."[4]

Things get even more challenging when customers connect across channels. As Leggett writes, "Often, transactional data and customer history are neither consistent nor consistently available across communication channels. Most companies have unintegrated communication channels: phone, email, chat, and web self-service." In 2014, only 36% of contact center decisions-makers told Forrester that their firms had an integrated system to deliver consistent experiences across channels.[5]

Unlike humans, virtual agents have no problem interfacing with multiple customer systems at the same time. Juggling multiple calls or chats at once is not a problem. As voice-based natural language understanding improves, the same system can deliver telephone or chat-based support, or support on any of the new platforms that are emerging, such as Apple Business Chat, Facebook Messenger, or Amazon's Alexa.

Virtual agents give the same right answer every time because they're programmed to do so. Even if conditions change due to a real-world event—a price cut, a new product, a competitor's offer, or even a breach of customer data—customer service managers can generate a new set of intents and answers that will ripple across all consumer inquiries, without having to retrain hundreds of reps.

Virtual agents don't sleep

Maintaining a customer service operation that's available 24 hours a day, seven days a week, is expensive. Most companies can't afford it.

But consumers can't necessarily ask their questions during regular business hours. We have working lives. We're not able to get on the phone to ask questions about our credit cards, our television service, or our airline reservations when we're working.

Often, people decide to handle nagging customer service problems on national holidays—exactly when agents are likely to have the day off too.

Providing service when human agents are not on duty isn't just a way of increasing customer satisfaction. It's got an upside in sales too. If your agent, real or virtual, is there to answer the question, she's also there to suggest a new product or upsell a service. Since you don't have to pay virtual agents overtime, that's an opportunity you can now afford to take advantage of.

Virtual agents scale

"Your call is important to us."

That's what the recording says while you're waiting. But the longer you wait, the less you believe it.

Unfortunately, in a typical contact center, there's no way to get around waiting.

If you happen to call or chat when the agents have time available, you're fine. But consumers don't behave like that. They bunch up their calls at lunchtime. They call at the beginning or end of their workdays. Or events may cause tie-ups. If there are thunderstorms across the northeastern United States, then airlines like JetBlue are going to see calls spike as people's flights are cancelled. Lord help you if it's the day before Thanksgiving.

Suppose a contact center must handle a load of 500 simultaneous calls or chats 80% of the time, between 500 and 700 10% of the time, and more than 700 in the remaining 10%. What's the appropriate staff level? If you said 700, the call center is wasting money on idle capacity four-fifths of the time. But if

you said 500, then the waits are going to get very long one hour out of every five.

The stakes are high. According to Forrester, 63% of US customers have stopped doing business with a brand due to poor customer service.[6]

This is an unsolvable problem until you add virtual agents into the equation. But for virtual agents, it's no problem to handle 500 calls, 700 calls, or 1,000 calls at once.

A contact center with capacity limitations must triage, disappoint customers who need to wait, overwork its staff at peak periods, or pay a premium to bring on extra agents at peak times. Scale matters to both quality of customer experience and cost. Virtual agents scale. People don't.

Virtual agents respond quickly

Is there anything more frustrating than waiting on hold for a customer service representative? Most of us would rather do anything else and only call customer service as a last resort.

A 2015 report by Consumer Reports found that 75% of people were highly annoyed when they couldn't get to a customer support representative on the phone, and 57% had become so frustrated with waiting for customer service that they'd hung up.[7]

The time to get an answer is a problem as well. If you try to get service through a chat interface, it sometimes seems as if there's no one on the other end of the conversation (in reality, the chat agent may be managing other chats simultaneously). And if you get someone on the phone, you may experience the dreaded "I'm waiting, but my computer isn't responding right now" instead.

Virtual agents have none of these problems. They pick up immediately. They answer immediately. From the customer's perspective, they're not just fast—they're snappy. This is a simple consequence of their ability to scale; computers generally don't

have to wait to find an answer, which means the customer doesn't have to wait to hear that answer.

Virtual agents make human agents better

No matter how effective your virtual agents are, customers will need to talk to people.

People are capable of empathy. Virtual agents aren't (at least they aren't credible at simulating empathy *yet*).

People are also capable of handling complex situations that virtual agents can't puzzle out. What happens when someone's bill is overdue, but she's been a customer for 11 years, and she calls and asks for an extension because someone in her house is sick, and her credit rating is good but has been declining, and she threatens to complain loudly and publicly on social media?

That's not an intent that a virtual agent is likely to be able to judge properly.

But that's not to say the virtual agent is useless is such situations. The virtual agent can quickly provide needed information to the customer representative handling the service request. The things that virtual agents are good at—like connecting with multiple customer systems, identifying intents, and recommending solutions—are still useful, even if it's a human agent on the phone to whom they're supplying this information.

At KLM Royal Dutch Airlines, for example, a virtual agent system trained on 60,000 customer service chat instances monitors agents' chats in the background and suggests answers.[8] And at the cable operator Charter Communications, customer service managers used cost and capacity savings from chatbots to fund a program to bring customer service jobs back from offshore to contact centers in the US, where agents were able to handle the most complex questions effectively.[9]

Virtual agents make companies smarter about their customers

Where are the problem areas in your business? Your customers know. Your contact centers are gathering that information every day. But can you get access to what they're learning? Drawing information back out from the aggregate experience of a customer service operation is a pretty tough thing to do, especially when customer needs are shifting hour by hour and week by week.

You need two things to access that customer intelligence: digital interactions and machine learning.

Digital interactions such as chat logs—and the records of intent left behind when virtual agents interact in either chat or phone channels—are the raw data for this analysis. Machine learning allows the same intelligent system that predicts intent to search for insights in the shifting patterns of customer requests and answers.

As Mike Pace explains it, "In the aggregate, successful customers may behave one way, and unsuccessful customers a different way. Digital channels allow you to figure out the patterns." From there, you can make changes, not just in how you do customer service but in how you design, describe, and price your products and services to head off the problems you've identified.

You can also monitor shifts in customer language and tweak chat or voice responses to mirror them. You can identify sources of frustration—like exclamation points, curse words, or all-caps typing—and then route those customers to agents who have proven better at empathy.

My conversation with Michelle Moore, head of digital for Bank of America and winner of American Banker's 2016 Digital Banker of the Year Award, shed some light on how to look at the evolution of a virtual agent system. When the company rolled out its voice- and text-based virtual agent Erica as part of the Bank of America mobile app, Moore learned that customers had 2,000 different ways of expressing the idea that they wanted to move money

around or send it to another person. Erica is evolving quickly to learn from customer interactions. "The cost of mining data from a system like this is cheaper," Moore told me. "You can see it in the conversation. There are patterns in what consumers are asking." By examining those patterns, Bank of America was able to react and improve quickly, using what Moore described as a tighter feedback loop. Since Erica was integrated into the company's app, website, and 800 number, it created an experience that behaved as consumers expected, where all the channels were connected.

Moore's experience reveals one of the most important benefits of virtual agent systems: with them, you can improve the *pace* at which your customer service operation evolves and improves. Virtual agent systems not only surface insights but allow you to test different approaches to applying those insights. This is why Dish Network's 40% rate of virtual agent-only answers to the intents it's currently covering will naturally improve—because week by week and month by month, people like Lucky Rai are learning more about how to get the system closer to optimal performance.

Virtual agents are channel-independent

Virtual agent systems are conversational systems. Their components don't depend on the interface where they're hooked up.

A single set of intents and responses can power a chat interface or a voice interface. Those same frameworks can work regardless of whether the customer is sending text messages, on a website, or interacting through a platform like Apple Business Chat. They can even power responses through a platform like Facebook Messenger or Amazon's Alexa, provided—as I discuss in chapter 6—that you can identify who the customer is.

Your customer service road map might allow for a virtual agent system to go in now for chat in an app (like Bank of America's Erica), text conversation on a website (like Dish Network), or

voice conversation on a phone line (like Avis Budget). But once you've engineered that system, the amount of effort required to port it to a different environment is far less than it took to create it in the first place.

This means that your customers can have the same fast, consistent experience regardless of how they contact you. That's efficient for you and reassuring for them.

To see how some of these advantages apply in practice, let's take a look at the experience of a large company in Sweden whose virtual agent system is rapidly improving.

The diverse benefits of a virtual agent system

According to its website, SEB is "a leading Nordic financial service group with a strong belief that entrepreneurial minds and innovative companies are key in creating a better world." That description gives you a pretty good idea of why the company was interested in investigating new customer technologies like virtual agents.

Nicolas Moch, a senior IT executive at SEB, describes what attracted him to the idea this way: "We knew we were going to have virtual assistants and robots as part of our workforce in the next few years. We wanted to learn quite fast by being an early innovator."[10]

Moch began by testing virtual agents internally with the company's IT help desk, answering employees' questions and solving problems like password resets. When that went well—reducing wait times and allowing IT help desk staff to focus on more sophisticated questions—Moch and his team decided to create a version of the agent system, called Aida, to answer customers' banking questions.

As Moch explained to me, SEB started by training Aida as they would an employee, teaching it how to answer some of the most

common questions. Starting in late 2016 and continuing to the present day, Aida has gained new capabilities. Now she can help you get a replacement credit card, lock your account if the card has been stolen, or even set up an appointment with a financial advisor to help you get started with investing.

Moch advises companies considering virtual agent deployments to examine multiple sources of value because, as he explains, "Cost reduction is not going to be sufficient—and there are effects that you don't see at first." These include having an agent available any time, day or night, and not funneling customers seeking service into a queue. "Our time to answer and time to resolution has gone down," he told me.

Aida helped SEB cope with a significant challenge in 2018: the rollout of the General Data Protection Regulation, or GDPR, the new European privacy regulations. As soon as a regulation like that comes into play, customer questions come pouring in. Aida enabled SEB to scale up and answer close to 10,000 additional questions.

For a bank, consistency is not just important; it's a matter of compliance. When you call a person, Moch estimates, you might get a different answer 10% of the time. But Aida gives the same answer every time.

Moch has found new ways to take advantage of Aida. The company is now implementing an algorithm to take notes when an agent talks to a customer. This note-taking will free the customer rep from note-taking tasks so they can give more attention to the customer, and it will also create a record that's useful as the relationship progresses.

But perhaps the most surprising outcome of SEB's virtual agent deployment was the reaction from the existing customer service reps. Like many companies in Europe, SEB had a unionized workforce, and Moch worried about how employees would react to a machine doing something that had been part of their jobs.

"We were very prudent with the [customer service] unions in this experiment," he said. "But it turns out that they were the people most motivated in working with this. They were the people asking the right questions. Guys in that position said, 'I'm 25, I will not answer these calls all my life. I would prefer to spend more time doing interesting stuff for the customer. Plus, I get the chance to work on a new technology.' They were working day and night with that system; they saw it as their futures. They were the first ones to see Aida as an extension of their jobs rather than as a replacement."

If you're planning a virtual agent deployment, pay attention to what Moch told me: "I advise not viewing cognitive tools as the ultimate cost-cutting tool because while it can help do that, the real value is the way it changes the way you operate."

A better way to think about virtual agents in customer service

It's time to stop the trend of cheaper service—and more frustrated customers—in the world of customer service. As the customer support call or chat becomes a bigger part of a customer's impression of the company, it's time to figure out how to do better.

But piecemeal approaches, such as throwing more customer service reps at the problem or adding still more digital systems for those people to access and manage, aren't going to solve the overall problem. With channels multiplying across phone calls, emails, chats, and platforms like Apple Business Chat, Amazon's Alexa, and Google Home, a more fundamental shift is in order.

Digital customer service demands an intelligent system that spans all these channels. It demands a system smart enough to connect to all the company's customer databases, one that answers questions on weekends and holidays, scales up to meet demand, and supports human agents when human agents are the best customer service solution.

Virtual agents built with artificial intelligence are the only technology that can do all these tasks. They're smart now and getting smarter and adapting with tight feedback loops.

If you keep doing customer service the old way, you'll just fall farther and farther behind. Virtual agents are the only way to keep up.

And as I'll describe in the next two chapters, they're ready—not just for customer service but for sales and employee communication challenges as well.

Chapter 4

THE CHALLENGE OF CONVERSATIONAL COMMERCE

Sherif Mityas wants you to buy more burgers, ribs, and wings—and he thinks a chatting robot is just what might get you in the mood.

Mityas is a senior executive at TGI Fridays, the casual dining franchise that would be delighted to show you a great time at one of its 870 restaurants worldwide. But the restaurant chain faces a demographic challenge: millennials, an important target market, are increasingly focused on convenience and are spending less time at casual dining restaurants.[1]

TGI Fridays wasn't going to take this shift sitting down. Its CEO, Ron Palleschi, told *Nation's Restaurant News*, "It's the millennial mind-set that I'm particularly interested in—the young at

heart for all of us, whether you are in that specific age group or you are 75 and you have an iPhone."[2]

Part of that appeal means reaching out where millennials prefer to interact. That means places like Facebook Messenger and Twitter, along with smart speakers like Amazon's Alexa Echo or Google Home. So Mityas—who started as Fridays' CIO in 2016 and is now the company's chief experience officer—set out to make it easier for everyone, including millennials, to converse with Fridays in their favorite places.

The thinking behind this strategy goes much further than just putting up a web form so folks can order online or make a reservation. "For us, this is an opportunity to think differently about how we engage with guests who talk to us," says Mityas. "Our guests like interacting. So we wanted to put fun things in. It can't just be mechanical, it has to be in the brand voice, because we are a fun and social brand."

None of Mityas's plan was going to work, though, unless it was wired into Fridays' transactional systems. The preparation for that took about a year. "Hooking it up was difficult," he says. "It was a ton of work from a digital perspective, connecting to internal POS [point-of-sale] systems, kitchen systems, waitlist systems, and payment systems." It also meant getting help from partners to put some artificial intelligence into the chatbot so it could customize its responses to be more fun and helpful based on customers' history of interacting with it.

Once it was hooked up to platforms like Facebook Messenger and Twitter, though, it began to pay off in a big way.

Fridays doubled its off-premises orders in a twelve-month period, growing that portion of its business by about $150 million per year.[3] Fridays' engagement on social media platforms increased by a factor of five. Millennials—and people who think like them—want their brands to connect in their favorite channels, and TGI Fridays' decision to be present in those channels with an on-brand

chatbot available day or night is generating significant benefits.

Mityas cites three factors in his and his company's ability to embrace these new technologies to move the needle on sales and with customers:

1. They started small. Mityas suggests creating a small pilot program around very specific use cases, like starting in a small market, or with a small subsegment of offers. And, as he recommends, "Measure the hell out of everything" to prove that it's worth doing.

2. They got the help they needed. "We sell ribs and beer; we don't have MIT scientists on staff," Mityas says. Find the partners with expertise in AI, commerce, systems integration, and chatbot intelligence who can get your bots working. This is not a do-it-yourself project.

3. They didn't lose track of what they were trying to accomplish. For TGI Fridays, that was the best guest experience, not "bots for bots' sake." You'll need a real use case that's more convenient, more helpful, or faster than your current real-world or digital channels. At Fridays, that meant making takeout orders and reservations easy for millennials on the go.

While there are lots of chatbots out there, few are actually delivering on the promise of commerce the way TGI Fridays' bots are. That's one reason why Mityas and his team were recognized as one the world's top one hundred IT organizations by *CIO* magazine for two years running. His moves were bold but never lost focus. As Mityas told me, "You have to be careful how you invest; it can be very cool, but to be economically viable, it has to have a return on investment."

The commerce chatbot gold rush

Sherif Mityas's experience at TGI Fridays is an encouraging sign for chatbot-based commerce, or, as it's come to be known, "conversational commerce."

Unfortunately, his experience is far from representative of all the people who've jumped on the chatbot idea. If fact, most of those who attempted to follow the path blazed by TGI Fridays are finding it a lot harder than it looks.

That's why, in this chapter, I'm going to start by dismantling the commerce hype about chatbots—separating what's been promised from what's actually been delivered. I'll show you what people are doing wrong. Then I'll show you what you will have to do to realize the promise of commerce driven by virtual agents.

Start with the hype. It surged into high gear in April 2016, when CEO Mark Zuckerberg kicked off the chatbot gold rush with an announcement, at the F8 conference, that the social network was opening up its Messenger platform to chatbot developers. Companies could create Messenger bots and encourage Facebook users to converse with them.

By 2018, more than 100,000 bots were up and running on Facebook Messenger.[4] And as always, when a new platform arrives, the focus was on gaining attention first and then somehow figuring out how generate sales later.

There was no shortage of pundits bullish on the idea of conversational commerce. Ezra Firestone, CEO of eCommerce trends tracker Smart Marketer, said that bots "will make eCommerce support WAY more efficient." Generation Z expert Tiffany Zhong, CEO of Zebra Intelligence, enthused, "I think chatbots and voicebots may be the future of commerce, as it relates to Gen Z. . . .What better way [to optimize for efficiency in shopping] than interacting and shopping via chatbots and voicebots?"[5]

Facebook's Andrew Kritzer, product manager for the Messenger platform, told *Chatbots Magazine*, "Messaging helps busi-

nesses and their customers connect in a personal and productive way—all at scale."

Capgemini actually estimated that spending via digital assistants would reach 18% of total retail commerce by 2021.[6]

This is sheer optimism, which is never a good business strategy. You're not just going to put a chatbot on Facebook or Amazon's Alexa and watch the orders pour in.

In fact, according to The Information, unnamed insiders at Amazon revealed in 2018 that only 2% of all owners of Amazon smart speakers had made a purchase, and 90% of that group had yet to make a second purchase from their devices. As one person who had been briefed on internal shopping numbers at Amazon said, "Clearly, voice shopping is not yet in the stage of being a mass market product."[7]

As it stands now, conversational commerce is one of a hundred shiny objects that marketers, retailers, travel companies, financial services companies, and anyone else who does business online is hearing pitches about.

So which is the future: Sherif Mityas's success at Fridays or all the chatbots on Messenger and Alexa that aren't generating much actual commerce?

To answer this, let's take a closer look at what has actually succeeded, what has failed, and what it would take to make money in this channel.

There are some notable modest successes with commerce chatbots

Outside of TGI Fridays, are people buying anything through interactions with chatbots? There are a few early and encouraging successes.

Sephora's Messenger bot will set up an appointment for you at a local Sephora store, where they can help you find the ideal

combination of makeup and skin products; its connections to local stores' appointment systems increased its success in booking appointments by 11%.[8]

Flowers and gifts retailer 1-800-Flowers set up a bot called GWYN (short for "Gifts When You Need") that works both on its site and on Facebook. You tell it what you're seeking and why (for example, chocolates for your mother), and it pops up some pictures of products that match. Chris McCann, president of 1-800-Flowers, told the publication *Digiday* that over 70% of the company's Messenger chatbot orders have been from new customers, and that these new customers skew younger than the company's traditional customer base.[9] You can try it yourself at https://www.1800flowers.com/gwyn-1800flowers.

There are other quirky examples of bots delivering results that, strictly speaking, fall somewhat outside of the definition of "commerce." The DoNotPay bot helped 160,000 Londoners get out of parking tickets through a simple conversational interface.[10] And the Hello Vote bot, a conversational tool used by Democratic parties to help people register to vote, helped 70% of those connecting with it to complete their registrations, compared to 40% for other typical online registration methods.[11]

But these simple chatbots have limits. They're based on a predetermined set of responses and decisions. I call them "path-bound" bots, since they work best with customers willing to follow the chatbot's optimal path very closely. If your consumer stays on that limited path, they can get her to an appropriate solution—the right flower bouquet or making an appointment at Sephora. But basically they're designed to handle only one intent.

Josh Bernoff, my cowriter on this book, ran smack into the limitations of that approach recently when he tried out the messenger bot for the travel reservation site Expedia. Josh wanted to make a very simple travel reservation: fly from Boston to New York (a

one-hour flight) and return on the same day. Here's a transcript of the conversation with Expedia's reservation chatbot:

Expedia: You can book or manage a trip on the go! How can we help?

Manage My Trips

Search Flights

Search Hotels

Search Activities

Daily Deals

[Josh clicks on "Search Flights."]

Expedia: Great! Let's get started on your flight search. Where are you flying to?

Josh: new york

Expedia: I found a few different cities that match your request. Did you mean of these?

[This was Expedia's response exactly as shown, including a missing word.]

New York, NY

New York, NY

If not, please type the city name again with the state or country. You can type something like 'Tokyo, Japan' or 'Paris, France.'

Josh: new york, ny

Expedia: I found a few different cities that match your request. Did you mean of these?

New York, NY

New York, NY

If not, please type the city name again with the state or country. You can type something like 'Tokyo, Japan' or 'Paris, France.'

[Josh clicks on the first of two identical options, "New York, NY."]

Expedia: We're sorry. We cannot search for the same arrival and departure locations.
Choose one:

Departure City

Arrival City

[Josh clicks on "Arrival City."]

Expedia: Where are you flying to?

Josh: New York, NY

Expedia: I found a few different cities that match your request. Did you mean of these?

New York, NY

New York, NY

If not, please type the city name again with the state or country. You can type something like . . .

[Josh clicks on the first of two identical options, "New York, NY."]

Expedia: We're sorry. We cannot search for the same arrival and departure locations.
Choose one:

Departure City

Arrival City

[Josh clicks on "Departure City."]

Expedia: Where are you flying from?

Josh: boston

Expedia: Ok, when do you want to leave?

Josh: october 17, return on october 17

Expedia: Is this flight roundtrip or one way?
Choose one:

One way

Round trip

[Josh clicks on "Round trip."]

Expedia: OK, when do you want to return?

Josh: october 17

Expedia: Dates entered [October 17, 2018 to October 17, 2018] are wrong
Choose one:

Departure date

Return date

Josh: you're pretty stupid

Expedia: OK, what city do you want to stay in?

Obviously, this chatbot is buggy and poorly designed. But even if you fixed the bugs, using it wouldn't be very helpful because it's path bound. It expects you to follow a rigid path for booking a flight, but real people booking flights don't follow rigid paths. They may be thinking of the dates, where they're leaving from, where they're heading, which airlines they have status on, which airlines they hate, how much they can spend, whether they insist on a window seat or an exit row, or any of a dozen other possible attributes of that flight. Where they start and what they do next is highly variable.

The biggest problem for this chatbot, of course, is that there's already a much better interface for booking a flight: the Expedia website or online app. True, narrowing down to your favorite flight options on the site or app can be tedious, but at least you can punch everything in and tweak the settings until you see the flight that's right for you.

This fact—that in many use cases, apps are easier to use than conversations—is why there is no Uber bot. Uber's app is so well designed for its purpose that a conversational interface would just slow things down and frustrate the person whose only goal is to get from here to somewhere else.

These simple, path-bound chatbots are generally no better

than the web forms and mobile apps they're trying to displace. Analyst Julie A. Ask explains it clearly in her Forrester Research Report called *Consumers Want Convenience, Not Conversations.* As she writes, "Digital business leaders should only build conversational interfaces where they offer more convenience than existing means of interacting with customers. . . . [Consumers] don't want conversations with brands; they want to complete tasks easily and efficiently and feel confident and valued while doing so."[12] Brands would like to engage consumers in conversation—that's the promise of Facebook Messenger for Business and Apple Business Chat. But those conversations will go nowhere unless the consumer perceives them as useful.

Forrester Research surveyed mobile development executives globally to assess just how many of them were on board with connecting up to third-party platforms like Facebook Messenger or Amazon's Alexa. In 2016, just after the gold rush began, 29% of the executives surveyed strongly agreed that they were developing a strategy to engage customers on those platforms. Just one year later, in 2017, that proportion had dropped to 18%.[13]

Ratnakar Lavu, CIO of a large American retail chain, explained some of the challenges standing in the way of chatbot development. "Some of the limitations with early bot platforms were that a lot of them talked about AI, but it still required a significant amount of effort in setting up rules. If you don't define the rule property, the result would be a bad situation for the customer, because the bot doesn't know how to deal with it." That sounds a lot like the pothole that Expedia's bot has ended up in.

If it sounds like I'm dumping on bots now, actually I'm not. It's just that by prematurely joining the Messenger chatbot gold rush, a lot of companies have found that their path-bound chatbots can't actually serve the customers any better than they could with their existing applications.

These conversations are happening in the wrong place. If a

customer wants to consider commerce with a company, it helps if she starts on the company's site or app rather than in a place like Facebook Messenger or Amazon's Alexa. Those platforms require a whole set of negotiations among the company, the platform, and the customers, which adds complexity to the relationship and makes it harder to give the customer what she's seeking: to buy or arrange something with the company. They lack the context that comes from knowing the consumers' history with the company. (I explain these challenges in more detail in chapter 6, which explores how companies can work effectively with conversational platforms like Facebook Messenger.)

And because they're path bound, they don't work the way customers expect. An airline reservation might start with the date, or the destination, or a requirement that the customer fly on the airline where he's about to achieve another status tier. Someone seeking gifts might want to start with a price range, an idea of who the recipient is, or a preference for the color pink. Path-bound conversations will never satisfy people who like to follow their own paths—and who doesn't? Only artificially intelligent systems can deal with people following their own paths.

Customer service virtual agents will evolve to do commerce

The chatbot gold rush is failing because it is starting in the wrong place. Path-bound chatbots attempting to sell are an annoyance, not a help.

So if you're interested in conversational commerce, I urge you to think differently. You should start by thinking about service, not sales.

As we saw in the last chapter, virtual agents—intelligent chatbots—can do a good job of improving customer service. What's the difference between sales and customer service?

Well, in customer service, the customer has questions, and the service agent's job is to get the customer the necessary answers, or solve the customer's problem, as soon possible.

In sales, the potential customer also has questions. The sales agent's job, just like the customer service agent's, is to answer the potential customer's questions and solve problems. But now the endpoint is not just getting the potential customer off the phone; the sales agent is supposed to sell her something.

Even though the process is similar, the attitude is different. Service managers worry more about efficiency, while sales managers worry about yield—about how many sales are closed and for how much.

But imagine for a moment that we applied the service mentality in a sales situation, and think about what that would mean for the process of automating parts of the agent's job.

In a sales situation, if we could design a virtual agent that would answer questions and get the customer quickly and efficiently into a state of mind where she could buy, yields would go up and costs would go down. We could leverage the selling techniques of the best salespeople and apply them. The potential customers would be happy because they would waste less time. The company would be happy because sales would be more efficient. Even the salespeople could be happier because they would get called into sales situations that were actually complex and emotional rather than rote and annoying. They could use their sales skills for the tough problems rather than the routine ones.

Just as in service, the automation of sales—and commerce—requires a sophisticated design. It requires virtual agents that use artificial intelligence to answer questions and guide customers to completion. Those agents would have to be far more sophisticated than the rigid path-bound chatbots that proliferated in the gold rush. *That's* why conversational commerce has not taken off yet—because the chatbots are not sufficiently sophisticated to do

all the sales tasks that a potential customer needs. If you're selling burgers and beer—and if you're as talented as Sherif Mityas—you might get lucky with a path-bound chatbot. But in general, you're going to need a virtual sales agent that's got a lot more intelligence.

A virtual sales agent that would work in these sales situations would need these qualities:

- **It understands natural language.** Because customers ask for the same thing in many different ways.

- **It's aware of context.** It knows the customer's history and uses that information to make appropriate recommendations. It doesn't ask questions or collect information if the answer is already in the system.

- **It follows the customer's desired path.** It allows people to ask questions and volunteer content in the order they are comfortable with rather than in a rigid flow determined ahead of time.

- **It has access to all product information.** It can tap into all product information systems within the company to determine the answer to questions like, "Is it available in red?" or "What time does the flight land?" or "Does this hotel have an indoor pool?"

To see how different this experience might be, let's revisit the Expedia flight reservation chatbot. Only this time, I'll create an imaginary virtual agent that's smarter (call it "Expedia Plus"). Here's what a transcript might look like:

Expedia Plus: How can I help you today?

Josh: Flight reservation.

Expedia Plus: OK, Josh, let's make a flight reservation. Can you tell me the dates and destinations?

Josh: I want to fly to Spokane on October 22.

Expedia Plus: Are you flying out of Boston, as you usually do?

Josh: Yup.

Expedia Plus: When are you coming back, or is this one-way?

Josh: I'll be back on October 25.

Expedia Plus: There are 20 flight options on the way out. There are no nonstops, but some have one or two stops. The prices vary from $573 to $889, and the durations from 9 hours 3 minutes to 16 hours 7 minutes. How would you like to narrow it down?

Josh: Pick flights with one stop. Keep the total time to 12 hours max. No red-eyes. And for Lord's sake, no basic economy class!

Expedia Plus: We've narrowed it down to 4 flights. Three are on American Airlines, where you have Platinum status, and one is on Alaska.

Josh: Do any of the flights get in before 8 at night?

Expedia Plus: Sure, here's the full list:

October 22 $615
AA 1094 Boston to Dallas 2:14pm–5:34pm
56 minutes stop in Dallas
AA 2086 Dallas to Spokane 6:30pm–8:17pm

October 22 $634
AA 2260 Boston to Phoenix 6:15am–9:13am
1 hour 1 minute stop in Phoenix
AA 455 Phoenix to Spokane 10:14am–1:01pm

[Josh clicks on first flight.]

Expedia Plus: The return flights at this price leave between 6:08am and 8:15am.

Josh: Show me the one that leaves at 8:15.

Expedia Plus:

October 25 $615
AA 829 Spokane to Phoenix 8:15am–11:23am
1 hour 8 minutes stop in Phoenix
AA 2320 Phoenix to Spokane 12:31pm–8:23pm

Josh: Go ahead and book it on my usual Mastercard. And request an upgrade.

Expedia Plus: I'll request a first-class upgrade based on your status. But if that doesn't come through, you can still upgrade to economy plus for $30. Do you want me to do that?

Josh: Yes, add that on.

Expedia Plus: Do you want me to arrange a hotel or rental car as well?

Josh: Not right now. Send me a message next week and let's take care of that then.

Expedia Plus: Safe travels, Josh. Happy to help.

Why is this bot actually better than the Expedia website? It lets you go down the path that you want. It understands who you are based on your history. It's basically an intelligent layer between you and the many systems that make up the air-travel world.

In other words, it behaves as a human travel agent would, if such an agent could have instantly responsive access to every computer system you need to evaluate flight choices and book a flight.

In the late 1990s, Shikhar Ghosh, the founder of Open Market, coined the term "human modems" for agents who sat in front of information consoles while they talked with customers on the phone.[14] He was making the point that the web would make many such jobs obsolete as soon as companies figured out how to put those information systems online where people could interact directly with them.

He was right, for the most part. But some of the information systems are still so complex that they require expert humans to navigate them. Many of those sales agents are basically functioning as human modems. As virtual agents get smart enough, they'll take over those connections too—sometimes by helping sales agents in the background and sometimes by completing transactions. Virtual agents will become our intermediaries and helpers in connecting to interconnected systems in complex sales situations.

When they do, they'll deliver an experience that's *superior* to a web form or app. And until companies start to embrace experiences like this for sales, conversational commerce attempts will

fail more often than they'll succeed because consumers won't be getting anything new and useful out of them.

Where conversational commerce will take off

Now that we've seen what it takes to succeed with conversational commerce—a customer service–like attitude rather than a focus on path-bound chatbots—we can figure out where it's going to appear first.

As cool as Sherif Mityas's success at TGI Fridays is, the answer is not "in the restaurant business."

Conversational commerce will succeed where people know they want to buy something but need some help navigating a complex purchase process. It's worth noting that such sales processes are usually in the same place that complex customer service needs exist as well. So conversational commerce will take off first in places where virtual agents are well suited for customer service questions as well.

These successes will begin in four key industries: travel, retail, telecom, and B2B.

Virtual travel agents will succeed by connecting with travel information systems

With the Expedia Plus example, you've already seen how a virtual agent could simplify the process of making a complex travel choice.

Many other travel choices are similar. For example, a hotel company could help you figure out the right balance between price, location, and features or amenities, such as an indoor pool or a four-star rating on TripAdvisor. You could have a conversation with the hotel company's virtual agent, just like Josh had his conversation with the imaginary Expedia Plus agent.

Travel companies are starting to embrace virtual agents for

service already. For example, at one hotel chain, a virtual chat agent on the site can help you with resetting your password, getting a receipt for a previous stay, and answering questions about restaurant hours or airport shuttles. And according to Forrester Research, KLM delivered 50,000 boarding passes via Facebook Messenger in its first three weeks of offering the option, and since March 2016, it has logged more than 1 million messages when counting booking confirmations, check-in notifications, boarding passes, and flight-status updates.[15]

Travel companies have exactly the right kind of customers for conversational commerce: customers who are saying, "I want to buy, but I need more information."

In retail, virtual salespeople will help customers narrow down choices

Like travel customers, retail customers often know they want to buy. They just aren't sure *what* to buy.

Who among us hasn't had the experience of looking at a site like Amazon.com or Bestbuy.com and wondering, "Which of these dozens of products is the right one for me?"

This is why 1-800-Flowers's GWYN chatbot is so successful—when you know you want to buy your sweetie something special (but not too expensive), it helps you narrow down the choices.

Conversational commerce in retail is already taking off in China. Alibaba's Taobao and Tmall apps used AI-based product recommendations to create 60 billion personalized shopping pages for customers. During China's Global Shipping Festival in 2017, Alibaba's virtual chatbot handled 95% of customer service questions.[16]

Ratnakar Lavu, the retail CIO who I mentioned earlier, suggests that virtual agents will help you narrow down intent. If you search for black shoes, the agent will know enough to ask why you need them—for casual strolling or a formal party. "I see that as

the most complex of the problems—knowing the right questions to ask," he says. "Once we get the intent, I have systems on the back end, I know your local store, and I can actually show you all the formal black shoes in your local store."

Retail companies typically have sophisticated product information systems that include every possible attribute of the thousands of products they offer. It's hard to search such systems: you can't easily get online access to such a system to ask, "Is there a table that's between five and six feet long, made of wood, costs less than $1,500, seats eight, and would fit with my early American décor?" But if the information is in these systems, a virtual agent can find it. Such interactions will probably evolve to be a lot like the Expedia Plus conversation, in which you help the system narrow down your choices based on a dozen different parameters that are unique to you, attributes that would be far too detailed to ever include on a web search form.

Telecom virtual agents will close the deal—and help with the upsell

As I've shown in previous chapters, virtual service agents helped create better customer experiences at companies like SiriusXM and Dish Network.

The distinction between sales and service in telecom is very fine. Every telecom sale is a consultative sale because telecom products are complex. A virtual agent on a company's website is the ideal helper to aid you as you decide between the Samsung and LG phones or among different programming packages in cable or satellite.

Telecom and pay TV companies are already the leaders in deploying virtual agents for service. Turning those agents to sales is a natural next step. At Dish Network, for example, virtual chat agents proved adept at helping people sign up for popular

pay-per-view events, such as boxing matches. Given the huge numbers of people calling in to sign up on the day of the fight, virtual agents are a natural way to expand the company's ability to handle the surge.

Look for telecom operators to become leaders in assisted selling too. They'll connect customers with the right packages in a consistent way, recommend upgrades, and reduce the time needed for customers to make complex choices as efficiently as possible.

Business-to-business sales are ripe for a virtual upgrade

If you're not in B2B, your caricature of a business-to-business salesperson is probably a little off. You may be thinking of a guy in a flashy suit who takes clients to dinner and plays golf with them. But most B2B salespeople are just folks who wait on the phone, listen to you describe the office supplies or machine tools or widgets you're looking to buy, and then navigate the company's systems to get your order placed properly.

Andy Hoar, a B2B sales expert and founder of the consultancy Paradigm B2B, has already predicted that millions of lower-skilled B2B salespeople would be displaced as B2B buyers opt for the convenience of ordering from self-serve online portals. And, as he told me, "I see a blurring of the lines in B2B between customer service and sales. More and more salespeople are providing advanced customer service while customer service representatives are increasingly selling basic products and services."

Where products are complex and service overlaps with sales, virtual agents make sense.

For example, Allstate's business insurance announced in 2018 a virtual agent called ABIE. Pronounced "Abby," from an acronym for "Allstate Business Insurance Expert," ABIE provides real-time answers about business insurance to small business owners. It doesn't sell insurance, but it does help you be smarter when you

talk to an insurance agent. (I talk more about how ABIE exemplifies the ways workers and bots are working together in the next chapter.) ABIE knows what it knows because it has digested countless Allstate insurance documents and used artificial intelligence to extract the answers to questions that small business owners most often ask.

It's a pretty good bet that the B2B salespeople of the future will be backing up and collaborating with virtual agents who are tapped into the detailed information about the complex products they are selling.

How to get started on conversational commerce

Conversational commerce creates a difficult strategic choice for most companies. On the one hand, it's clear that consumers, trained by the likes of Alexa and Siri and having interacted with virtual agents in customer service, will be ready for virtual salespeople. But it's also true that based on what's come before, plunging heedless into the chatbot gold rush is a mistake.

The keys for success here are visible in Sherif Mityas's story at TGI Fridays and in the successes at organizations like Allstate Business Insurance, 1-800-Flowers, and KLM.

First, don't look for transformational results right away. Conversational commerce will arrive slowly, and successes for most organizations will grow from a modest beginning.

Second, navigate politics carefully. Sales organizations have power and will balk at channel conflict. That's why it often makes sense to start with artificially intelligent assistants that empower sales staff, as Allstate Business Insurance did, rather than imagining that you're going to replace them.

Third, start small, as Mityas recommended, carefully measuring results of your initial efforts.

Fourth, build on successes in virtual agents for customer service, as Dish Network did. Look for opportunities to upsell consumers who already engage with you.

Fifth, recognize that hooking up your systems to bots is the hard part, because any chatbot is most useful only to the extent that it knows everything in your systems about both your customers and your products.

Sixth, you may be better off pioneering these efforts on your own site and apps, where customers are most likely to be ready to transact, before extending them into platforms like Apple Business Chat or Facebook Messenger.

But more important than all of these recommendations is an attitude. Customers don't want to chat with you just for fun. They're quite capable of using your well-developed web and mobile interfaces to buy simple things simply. The right place to start with conversational commerce is with challenges—like choosing the right hotel or selecting the perfect gift—that go beyond what simple interfaces can easily deliver.

Once you've chosen the right problem to solve, you'll be in a position to start succeeding. And as conversational commerce become more mainstream, you'll be positioned to grow your virtual sales agent program along with it.

Chapter 5

HOW BOTS AND PEOPLE WORK TOGETHER

Scot Whigham was between a rock and a hard place.

Whigham was the head of global IT service and support for InterContinental Hotel Group (IHG), the vast hospitality company that includes over 5,000 hotels, 800,000 guest rooms, and 30,000 employees. On any given day, any of those employees could be calling the IT help desk for a password reset, to untangle a technology issue, or to fix a computer problem. Whigham's IT services group included nearly 150 people, but it was reaching its limits. There was not enough budget—or enough space—to hire more help desk staff.

IHG needed a creative solution that would expand capacity without expanding its workforce. But as Whigham explained

it to me, "IGH is a people-oriented business." The hotel staffers calling the help desk had, in many cases, long relationships with the company. While automation of some kind could extend the capacity of the help desk workforce, how could the company improve efficiency without destroying those relationships? As Whigham put it, "We had to be very careful, very risk averse, in trying to go down this path."

So proceeding deliberately carefully, IHG's help desk began to explore a conversational interface that would add virtual agents to the IT help desk.

The company's first attempts were too limited and path bound. "We had a way of thinking about this technology that was an old mind-set," Whigham says. IHG tried to code every bit of conversation in scripts, but that approach didn't scale. People had too many ways of asking the same question. When the coders imagined the conversation would go a certain way, it often went differently in actual field tests. The result was not yet a good experience for the workers calling in.

So IHG tried a new approach. Instead of developers scripting out the flow, IHG used machine learning to review chat transcripts and build the framework based on the way human agents were answering employees' questions already. As Whigham told me, "The people who are currently answering the questions should be the people training the system. Those people get to reflect our organizational culture. And you can absolutely build culture into platform."

The result was a system that worked *with* the help desk staff instead of replacing them.

IHG's help desk can now scale to meet spikes in demand that might result from putting a new technology system or set of rules in place. The machine-learning-trained virtual agent can respond in multiple channels, including calls, chats, emails, and mobile text messages. "We can scale up to meet what comes into our

systems, but then scale down so that we don't have excess capacity that we are paying for," Whigham explained. Instead of paying extra staff in times of low demand, the organization can scale down and redeploy resources to perform other important things on the to-do list.

For the tasks that it was trained for, like password resets, the virtual agent system eventually ramped up to be able to handle 80% to 85% of the volume of questions coming in. And it keeps getting better. Workers who had worked with IHG for years helped with suggestions for improvements. Whigham added more and more possible intents to the platform so it could handle a wider variety of requests. Once it was trained on one of those intents, it could answer questions about that intent for dozens of users simultaneously, all over the world, at any time of day. No group of help desk staff could possibly get trained, adept, and consistent on a new topic so quickly.

The results were not only faster responses for routine inquiries but also more accurate service, which enabled IHG to run its business better. Every call or chat or text message was completely and accurately documented—and that documentation didn't swallow up any help desk worker resources.

Even when the virtual agents can't answer a question, they can help. The initial part of every help desk request is collecting basic information from the worker on the other end. The virtual agent system takes care of that, regardless of whether it's answering the question itself or handing it off to a help desk staffer. Even in those more complex and less routine cases that the virtual agent system can't handle, it's listening in the background, gathering material that will eventually make it easier to train it for more user intents.

Whigham reports that among hotel workers who have engaged with the system, satisfaction rates remain high. Workers can get answers quickly. They can talk to a person if they need to. They can connect on any convenient channel, from phones to text messages.

And the IT help desk at IHG is no longer between a rock and hard place—because it can do its job effectively with machines and people working together.

Workers do better with bots

IHG's hybrid help desk features workers and virtual agents—bots—working together. That is what the future will look like, with human workers who are helped, augmented by, and working side by side with machine intelligence.

Why? Because that's the most effective way to take advantage of what machines are good at and what people are good at.

As artificial intelligence researcher Hans Moravec first noticed in the 1980s, people and computers are good at very different things. In his book *Mind Children*, he wrote, "It is comparatively easy to make computers exhibit adult level performance on intelligence tests or playing checkers, and difficult or impossible to give them the skills of a one-year-old when it comes to perception and mobility." Since Moravec wrote that, computers have made great progress in perception and even mobility but remain crippled in recognizing emotion and exhibiting empathy.

A customer service rep of minimal competence can effortlessly diagnose when someone is frustrated and can quickly develop the instinct of knowing when to give a customer a break based on past history, value to the company, or just the fact that she is struggling to dig out from a snowstorm of historic proportions. Artificially intelligent virtual agents, on the other hand, are wizards at assembling data from disparate systems to render a judgment instantly, even if they lack the emotional intelligence to know *why* such a decision might be right.

As futurist and author Gerd Leonhard puts it, "Whatever is very simple for a human is very hard for a computer, and whatever is very hard for a human is simple for a computer."[1]

That's why the smartest companies are now inventing workflows where virtual agents and people work together. J. P. Gownder, Forrester Research's expert on artificial intelligence and the future of work, writes, "Intelligent machines can help employees by taking routine and annoying tasks off their plates, delivering insights at key moments, and freeing up time for them to focus on more interesting and valuable work."[2] And Gownder points the way to the best strategy here: "An easy route to augmenting employee performance with a technology like AI is to introduce it into existing tools and workflows."[3]

Shel Israel, the author of seven books about business strategy and the future, described for me how he believes the future of AI will unfold. "As we move into the AI century," he said, "there are going to be transformations in who does what. The future of work is that humans will do less of it. What we can never forget is to factor the humans into workflow and systems of every kind."

It's not just that the computers need help from humans on judgment and empathy. It's also that humans need help to be freed from the unending drudgery of rooting through computer systems to find information for people.

According to the Gallup polling organization, employees' engagement in their jobs is basically flat.[4] In 2014, the number of US employees who said they were "involved in, enthusiastic about, and committed to their work and workplace" was about one in three. Three years later, in 2017, the level of commitment remained basically unchanged at this pathetically low level. Fifty-one percent of employees are actively looking for a new job or watching for new job openings.

Information systems and regulation make life challenging for these staff. Forrester analyst Craig Le Clair takes the radical position that human-machine collaboration should start not with customers but with a more captive audience that needs a lot more help: employees. As he writes, "Employees live by complex rules,

particularly in regulated industries such as healthcare and wealth management. Workers now spend up to 30% of their time interacting with dozens of internal systems, knowledge repositories, and reporting apps. Wrestling with cumbersome systems consumes too much human talent."[5]

Historically, this attitude makes sense. People working with machines is nothing new. When the first spreadsheet VisiCalc entered the workplace in the 1970s, accountants with Apple IIs on their desks appeared smarter than the guy in the next office with a paper spreadsheet. "Management information systems" made executives smarter in the '80s. The internet and the web in the '90s and mobile devices in the 2010s have made all of us into enhanced humans, with instant access to every published fact and statistic. All of these systems have made us smarter, but navigating them is increasingly difficult. The next advance is clear. Virtual agents, navigating systems within our companies, can make us all better at our jobs.

Why not start with the corporate intranet?

When it comes to helping workers succeed, a great place to start is with workers within companies, searching for information or help. That's what IHG did with its help desk. And it's no wonder. Finding information within large companies is quite difficult. As HP's past CEO Lew Platt said, "If only HP knew what HP knows, we would be three times more productive."[6]

But knowledge management—the field dedicated to making corporate information available—has mostly failed. We replaced knowledge management systems with intranets, but people still have a hard time finding what they're looking for. As Steve Hamrick and Daisy Hamrick said in a *CMSWire* article called "Your Intranet Probably Sucks—and Here's Why," "[O]dds are your intranet is killing your company's chances at staying lean

and agile. Your employees can't find what they're seeking. They spend an inordinate amount of time clicking through pages that are either outdated or contain incorrect information. They waste an hour or more each day searching for the right information." Any of us who has searched fruitlessly through the corporate intranet knows this is true.

The problem is search. It's just not the right interface. Why not ask a bot to find what you're looking for?

That's just what we did at my company, [24]7.ai. Our marketing and sales staff needed help finding the right information. So we created a chatbot called "Yoda" that finds the wisdom they're looking for. People dive into it and ask questions all the time—it responds with the document or answer most likely to be helpful, whether that's the company's best sales PowerPoint and accompanying video or a description of how we organize the sales department. In fact, 70% of the time, when Yoda provides an answer, the employee says it's done a good job. Yoda is helping these workers avoid a lot of wasted time mucking about in the intranet with a search function that might or might not surface the answer they're looking for.

Stories like this are popping up all over.

- Bupa, a health insurer and health care company that serves over 15 million customers, was planning a major office move in London. So it created Cyan, a chatbot designed to help with the flood of move-related questions. Cyan could answer questions as varied as "What's the closest tube station to the new office?" and "How do I contact payroll?" After the move was complete, the company expanded it to answer questions about the new office, including the popular "What's the guest Wi-Fi password today?" Bupa's senior digital communications manager, Del Green, manages the chatbot. "Employees

are intrigued by Cyan," he says. "We already see many opportunities to expand our use of chatbots at Bupa."[7]

- At the Swedish financial services company SEB, the customer-facing virtual agents that I describe in chapter 3 were actually the second stage of a project that began with virtual agents on the company's help desk. The help desk virtual agents were able to reset passwords, unlock Microsoft Active Directory accounts, and point employees to the right IT services solution. The virtual agent system was able to handle 50% of the calls by itself. After the company added more intents to the agent system's capabilities, that rate improved to 70%. Service was faster and more consistent. On Monday mornings, a particularly busy time, call resolution times dropped from 20 minutes to four minutes or less.

- At Brazil's Bradesco Bank, a virtual agent has eliminated 90% of the 2,200 calls the company's help desk receives every day. It responds to 200,000 possible questions that support many of its 59 products.[8]

These kinds of systems can make employees a lot more productive. But what about workers that are helping customers? To give them the help they need requires a different level of automation. They need help from robots to actually get customer requests executed.

Employees (and virtual agents) need help from robotic process automation

This vision of people working with AI-driven helpers sounds great, but there's a problem.

The problem is the tangle of systems within every company.

Companies typically have multiple customer relationship management (CRM) systems. They may have separate systems for billing and customer service and sales. There are also likely systems for keeping track of products and their features and for inventory.

In an ideal world, all of these systems would be connected. But often, they're not. Some may be based in the internet cloud, while others run on servers that companies maintain. Some might require web interfaces, while others expect you to interact on Windows computers.

In chapter 8, on architecture, I'll describe how companies need to prepare their internal technology for the virtual agent future. But that's a long-term view. What do you do about the challenge of actually getting stuff done now with corporate systems that don't interoperate?

For example, consider the plight of the employee who needs to take an order, cancel an order, or check on an order for a customer. That worker might need to touch five different systems to complete the work. Shipping that product might require updating the CRM systems, sending an order to a warehouse somewhere, and decreasing the inventory after the company ships something to the customer.

That's a lot of work for an agent to do. It's time consuming, and it's easy to make a mistake.

Integrating the systems—linking them together—might take years and millions of dollars. In the meantime, you've got people acting as the human glue that holds the whole thing together.

The idea behind robotic process automation, or RPA, is pretty simple. It just automates the combination of tasks a worker might need to do, without all the usual need to code the application program interfaces (APIs) that allow systems to interoperate. A typical RPA application might touch five applications and automate up to 500 clicks that otherwise a human might have to do manually.

And for people and virtual agents alike, it's a huge time-saver.

Without RPA, in a given company, a virtual agent system might automate 20% of the possible intents. RPA could help increase that number to 80%. That's the difference between a virtual agent being a small help and being a hugely powerful productivity driver.

RPA systems are becoming more sophisticated. They can connect web applications, Windows applications, and even more primitive form-based systems. They can identify places on the screen that require clicks or inputs and put the required data in the right spot.

In itself, RPA is just a sort of lubricant that makes the whole system work better—it makes people more productive and gives virtual agents the ability to actually execute across multiple systems. In the long run, any business that's using RPA will eventually have to integrate its systems together the robust way, with APIs.

But when it comes to charging up the productivity of people and machines working together—and not waiting for IT and its systems integrators to fix everything perfectly—RPA is a crucial element.

I spoke with Shail Khiyara, chief marketing and experience officer at Blue Prism, an RPA vendor with 1,000 clients ranging from Pfizer and Prudential to Coca-Cola. As he describes it, RPA allows companies to get "quick wins at enterprise scale." The reason? RPA allows companies to automate what previously was tough to automate: the connections between corporate systems. Put that capability in front of an agent, human or virtual, and that agent can deliver on the customer's intent a lot more quickly.

The bottom line is that RPA lets companies get pilot programs off the ground quickly by connecting systems without the need for coding. It allows agents to spend more of their time on actual customer-facing and complex activities rather

than using their intellect to navigate their way through all the companies' systems.

How virtual and human agents can serve customers together

There's no part of the business where virtual agents and real people can work together better than in helping customers. Bots are fast and accurate. People are empathetic and have judgment. Together they've got what it takes to deliver the best service possible.

But it's not as simple as creating a cube farm with a robot in every other seat.

Based on my and my colleagues' research on what customers are doing, we've identified three basic modes in which virtual and human agents work together: bots initiating the conversation and handing off to a person, human agents serving customers with help from bots, or bots serving customers with human agents supervising.

Bots that hand off to agents

In a sense, all of the examples from the first four chapters fit this mode of interaction. When a customer gets on the phone with a virtual agent or chats with one, there's always the possibility that the customer asks for something that the virtual agent can't provide. That might be a complicated case the virtual agent can't puzzle out. It might be a case where the customer indicates that they're upset (which virtual agents can often spot easily, because the customer uses curse words, exclamation points, starts shouting, or uses lots of words in all caps).

It might even be a case where the virtual agent hands off to human agents by design. Bots can easily collect information, such

as the customer's name or account number and a description of the problem, and suggest resolutions before handing the customer off to a person. (Touch-tone interactive voice response systems do this already, but bots are more efficient at it—and less annoying for the customer to converse with.) The human agent in this situation has a head start; she already knows whom she's talking to and what the question is, and the virtual agent can weave in other information, such as past history of product purchases, a service level, or a slot in the company's hierarchy of loyalty levels. For example, if a hotel customer service agent knows the customer on the line has stayed at the chain twelve times already this year—and has been a loyalty member for 15 years—she can move more quickly to resolve a problem with a reservation and keep that customer happy. Having the customer's background teed up by the virtual agent shortens the time to resolution and delivers the best possible experience.

Connor Cirillo, conversational marketing manager at the marketing services company HubSpot, shared an example of such a bot with me. HubSpot's chatbot qualifies leads, delivers content, and connects potential customers with HubSpot's (human) sales staff—all through Facebook Messenger. Leads that come from the chatbot are 33% cheaper than those from a traditional landing page, and the quality of those leads—measured by their willingness to engage with salespeople—is 40% higher.

Bots that whisper in agents' ears

Some companies aren't comfortable with their customers talking to virtual agents because they want to provide a human touch from the start. As a senior enterprise architect at professional services firm Marsh & McLennan told Forrester Research in its December 2016 report on AI in financial services, "We would never have a wealth management client interact with a robot."[9] But

that doesn't mean the agents themselves can't be smarter because a bot is whispering in their ear.

Bot-assisted customer service agents appear much smarter than agents who work alone. If there's a new discount, the bot brings it to the attention of the agent. If something's out of stock, or a new rule prevents the customer from accessing an offer, the agent will know that too. It's like having an assistant scurrying around to figure out the best things for you to say to the customer.

For example, the virtual agent I mentioned in the previous chapter that helps Allstate customers with business insurance, ABIE, actually started as an aid for salespeople. Allstate's independent insurance agents needed to find specific pieces of information that related to clients' businesses—like what it would take to insure a nonprofit for liability or how insurance costs might vary if a business crossed state lines. These facts were hard to access quickly because they were locked up in hundreds of separate documents. Questions tended to flood into the Allstate underwriter or sales support line, even if the information was available online. With the help of experts from Earley Information Science (EIS), Allstate built a virtual agent system, which was the first version of ABIE. ABIE was designed to answer common questions from insurance agents and now handles more than 25,000 inquiries every month. According to EIS, "ABIE is faster than phoning the call centers and has become the preferred way for agents to get help. . . . As a result, commercial policy sales have grown, and business stakeholders can rapidly publish FAQs and critical information, just in time."[10]

The Forrester report cited above shares a couple of other financial services companies using bots to help agents on the phone. For example, at one large insurance company, contact center reps were sometimes unsure whether their compliance department would allow them to handle certain kinds of calls, since they didn't have full insurance licenses. The reps now sent text messages to

a virtual agent system about whether—and how—to solve these customers' problems. As a senior project manager told Forrester, "Some reps adopted the machine easily, with a sci-fi mind-set, but others feared their average call time would suffer. It did not. First-call resolution, on the other hand, turned out to be 2% higher, from 88% to 90%."

And at a large global bank, bots help agents manage complex tasks like retirement rollovers or setting up new accounts. They text a virtual agent with issues like "I need to do a disbursement for [customer name], but he also wants to add a beneficiary." The virtual agent uses RPA to gather the data, fill out the needed forms, and upload them to the client portal.

Bots that work with agent supervision

If a new employee were working with customers on the phone, you might want to put a more experienced staffer on the phone at the same time, to look over his shoulder. That way the more experienced worker could step in if the new guy can't figure something out.

That's exactly how supervised bots work.

A human agent might supervise eight or ten chatbot conversations, far more than a human agent could handle if they were doing the talking. When a virtual agent gets stuck, the more experienced human can step in and solve the problem.

But the human has one more job: to tag the customer's intent, which the virtual agent may have missed. This information gets fed back into the virtual agent system and makes it a little smarter, so next time it can handle a similar interaction on its own. This is how supervised machine learning works and, over time, should reduce the need for human supervision.

In this mode of interaction, the virtual agents do what they do best—handle routine cases quickly and efficiently. And the humans

do what they do best—solve more complex problems, help people who need a little more empathy, and train the virtual agents on cases they're not yet ready to handle.

In future workplaces, help from bots will be commonplace

In 2000, it was unimaginable to work without a PC connected to the internet. Every knowledge worker had access to the collected intelligence of the web and the computing power of a desktop or laptop computer. We didn't call them "augmented workers"—this was just how people working with information did their jobs.

In 2015, it was unimaginable to work without a smartphone. Every knowledge worker had access to information instantly from the palm of her hand. We didn't call them "augmented workers"—this was just how people moving around did their jobs.

In 2025, it will be unimaginable to work without help from bots.

Here's why: search has reached its limits. People can't find things fast enough on intranets or corporation information systems. Whether they're updating information with human resources, getting help from the help desk, or working with customers, chatbots—virtual helpers—will be the only tool fast enough to deliver the information they need, support their decisions, and then execute processes robotically.

Where will this begin? Wherever it's needed most—and where processes are well defined and rule based. As Ashish Bansal, former senior director of data science and merchant products lead at the bank Capital One, told Kaleido Insights analyst Jessica Groopman, "Those in individual functions, groups, or teams are often the most acutely aware of the problems that can and should (or should not) be automated."

Companies need to prepare themselves for this future. Any group that interacts with customers or employees can become

more productive with the help of bots and RPA. But that shift will mean transitioning workers from following automated scripts to working with, training, and supervising bots.

Workers will need training to prepare for this future. But with the help of bots, they'll be able to help customers—and their fellow employees—a whole lot faster.

Chapter 6

THE TANTALIZING PROMISE OF CONVERSATIONAL PLATFORMS

Butterball is an American brand icon. Americans buy over 40 million turkeys every Thanksgiving, and more than one in three of them is a Butterball.

The beloved Butterball Turkey Talk-Line, where home cooks can call and get answers to any turkey question that's on their minds, is an essential feature of the brand. So when it came time to prepare the Talk-Line for the future of consumer communications, Kyle Lock knew he had to be very, very careful.

Lock has been with Butterball for 12 years. Currently the senior

director of retail marketing, Lock has helped pioneer many innovations for the company, like ready-to-roast turkeys in a bag, ground turkey, and smoked turkey sausages. But this challenge was different, because it touched the core of Butterball's iconic reputation for service.

Cooking a turkey for Thanksgiving can be tricky. Hosts need to buy the right size to feed a whole bunch of people who are likely to be visiting. They need to allow time for the bird to thaw so it's ready to stuff, baste, and cook. Cook it too long and it's dry and burnt; too short and the experience could be terrible. And it needs to come out at the exact right moment, when the family is arrayed around the table like a Norman Rockwell painting.

Historically, Butterball has solved home cooks' problems with the Butterball Turkey Talk-Line. Since 1981, you've been able to make a toll-free call and talk to an expert. Consumers make over 100,000 calls a year to the Talk-Line, and every single one reaches a real person—like Marge Klindera, an 81-year-old grandmother who is ready to walk them through any possible Thanksgiving challenge.

But now there are a lot of Amazon Alexa–powered smart speakers sitting in people's kitchens. When you've got both hands and a big turkey in the sink, it makes a lot of sense to turn to Alexa and ask for help. Butterball wanted to be there for customers in their moments of need.

Lock and his team started planning the Butterball Alexa skill more than a year before its November 2018 launch. "These kinds of decisions and projects are not taken lightly. Anything this close to the center of the brand must be planned out well in advance and as perfectly executed as possible," Lock told me. "As tech moves forward, the most important thing for us is not to degrade the experience, not to betray the foundation of the brand." As a result, Butterball made several important decisions in developing the Alexa skill.

The Alexa skill would need to easily answer the most popular questions on Butterball's site. When you say "Ask Butterball" to Alexa, it prompts you to ask questions about "planning, preparing, cooking, or enjoying a turkey." If you inquire about how long to cook an 18-pound turkey, it first asks if you're including stuffing (who wouldn't?) and then recommends a four-and-one-half to five-hour cooking time at 325 degrees Fahrenheit. Even though very few people deep-fry a turkey, a lot more are curious. "Deep frying is a great option, but you'll need to take a few precautions to do it safely," the Butterball skill recommends, and follows up with five deep-frying tips.

Another important decision that Lock and his team made was to have the Alexa device answer in the voices of actual Butterball Turkey Talk-Line experts rather than the familiar Alexa voice. For example, it's very reassuring to hear Marge's experienced and friendly voice telling you that the turkey is done perfectly when the temperature registered by a meat thermometer in the thigh reaches 180 degrees.

After a careful process, Butterball selected Mobiquity, a development shop expert in creating voice applications, to build the Butterball skill. The skill took six months to build, as Butterball and Mobiquity mined all of the Turkey Talk-Line's most common questions to build a giant tree of queries and responses. Because there are many ways to ask the same question, they developed the skill to be flexible in recognizing and responding to key words and synonyms. And together they developed folksy but informative conversational scripts for the responses and got three Turkey Talk-Line volunteers, including Marge, to record those responses, which you can now hear coming out of your Amazon Echo speaker.

Butterball then went all in on publicity. They promoted the Alexa skill with a big graphic on the top of their website and rolled it out with a PR push that generated over 1,000 articles

and national TV appearances on NBC's *Today* show and *ABC World News Now*.

Based on the response, Lock and Butterball have successfully brought their customer service operation into the future. Twenty thousand consumers have launched the skill and interacted with it. "The feedback we've gotten has been really positive," Lock says.

But the key is a new way of delivering service that is branded, helpful, and as personal and friendly as a phone call—crucial at the moment in the kitchen where the right decision can save a holiday.

Lock's advice for others is not to just build a generic skill, because there are thousands of them, and it's hard to stand out. "I think each brand needs to figure out how they can express themselves honestly and truthfully through the technology," he says. But when you're elbow-deep in a turkey, asking the Alexa device on the counter for help makes a whole lot of sense.

The promise–and challenge–of conversational platforms

Alexa is popular. People are talking to it on devices, just as they are asking Siri and Samsung's Bixby questions on their phones and Google Assistant questions in all sorts of places. And these are just the voice platforms. People are also chatting on messaging systems such as Facebook Messenger and Apple's iMessage. These are platforms—spaces maintained by large tech firms like Facebook, Apple, Amazon, and Google—where companies can build virtual agents and chatbots to help their customers, just as Butterball did.

Embracing these new, popular platforms seems like a no-brainer. But the deeper I got into investigating these platforms, the more I realized that conversational platforms aren't really ready to be that go-to solution for companies connecting with customers. The Butterball skill is a great success, but duplicating

that success is going to be challenging for most companies.

As I'll describe in the rest of this chapter, on these platforms as they're currently designed, challenges with authentication, privacy, user experience, and discovery are going to get in the way. The conversational platforms themselves are going to succeed just fine with consumers. But for quite a while, technical and business challenges are going to hamstring companies that hope to use these platforms to serve their customers.

Conversational platforms are taking off

People are chatting with machines in both text and voice channels at astounding rates. Let's look at text chat first.

Text chat platforms are embedded in our lives

A billion people use Facebook every day,[1] and at least in the US, they're spending about an hour a day there.[2] No single company has ever before swallowed up as much of people's time as Facebook has. As a result of Facebook's popularity, its messaging system, Facebook Messenger, is also embedded in people's lives. Messenger had 1.3 billion monthly users in 2017[3]—11% of the world's population—and continues to experience double-digit annual growth rates. Every day, there are over 8 billion Messenger conversations taking place.[4]

Messenger is a huge chat platform, but it's not the only one that matters. People send over 60 billion messages every day on WhatsApp.[5] Even more amazing is that people sent over 63 quadrillion (that's 63,000 billion) messages on Apple's messaging app iMessage in 2016.[6]

Are businesses meeting their customers on these chat platforms? They're beginning to. The TGI Fridays chatbot I described in chapter 4 is now one of 300,000 chatbots on Messenger.[7] But

are they effective? That's a more difficult question. For now, most of what we see is just herds of companies doing experiments.

Smart speaker devices have become a hot new category

Devices like Amazon's Echo and Google Home Mini face a challenge that text chat platforms don't—consumers have to buy them and set them up in their houses. Even so, the growth of this new category of electronics is incredible. Comscore estimated that in February of 2018, smart speaker devices were in 20% of US households with Wi-Fi, which meant that penetration had grown by an astounding 50% in just three months. And they're multiplying even within homes. Amazon announced that people had bought more than 100 million Alexa devices by the end of 2018.[8] Sales of Google Home have also accelerated; Strategy Analytics estimated that Google's market share in smart speaker sales had reached two-thirds of Amazon's, as of the second quarter of 2018.

What are people doing with these devices? Well, for the most part, they're playing music and asking questions rather than connecting with companies like Butterball.

I spoke with Tom Webster, the senior vice president at Edison Research, who conducted research on smart speakers for NPR. As he put it, "The word I would use to describe the activities that these kind of owners engage in is mundane." According to his company's survey for NPR, about 90% of smart speaker owners had requested their devices to play music.[9] The other common activities included "get the weather," "ask a general question," "set a timer/alarm," "get the news," or "tell a joke." Even these simple and obvious applications have endeared the speakers to their owners. (An editor at CNN who owned an Alexa device reported that the first four words her infant recognized were "mom," "dad," "cat," and "Alexa."[10] I have to wonder when "Alexa" will overtake "cat" and "dad.")

Why are these devices so popular? As John Trimble, chief revenue officer of the music service Pandora, wrote in Recode, “Simply put, voice-activated content sits right at the heart of what consumers want: Control.”[11]

Webster’s research for Edison and NPR included ethnographic studies in which researchers observed families interacting with their devices. As he told me, “These devices rapidly become an essential part of the everyday life of the people who own them. You just get so used to being able to do things hands free.”

With this level of consumer interest, companies are beginning to experiment. As of fall of 2018, Amazon reported that companies and startups had created 50,000 Alexa skills.[12] (As of January 2018, companies had developed 1,719 Google Assistant apps.[13]) In a 2017 Forrester Research survey of 148 marketers and business executives, 31% said they were piloting or planning to test Amazon Alexa skills, and 30% were doing the same for applications for Google Assistant.[14]

But these third-party apps are not nearly as popular as the music playback and simple tasks and questions that Alexa users got started with. In the Edison/NPR survey, only 22% of the respondents said they liked skills and features created by brands. As Forrester’s Rob Koplowitz and Andrew Hogan wrote in their 2017 report *Plan For Success in Conversational Computing*, “[T]he current state of conversational computing is limited. To reach a point where the computer can reliably understand and respond to you, interactions are almost always simplified to the point where they’re not useful. That’s why we see 100,000 Facebook Messenger chatbots and over 12,000 Amazon Alexa skills with extremely low uptake.”[15]

Sure enough, if you look at the charts for the best-rated applications, the leaderboard includes skills that play the sounds of frogs and rainstorms to help you sleep and quiz games you can play with your family. A perennial leader is a skill that makes fart

sounds. The best-rated financial services applications are celebrity coaching skills on careers or leadership.

Skills that actually perform transactions get low ratings. One out of three people who rated the Capital One banking skill gave it three stars or less—a terrible rating for Amazon. Here's a typical review, from user "John T.," of the Alexa skill for American Express:

> This skill works as advertised and is very easy to use and set up. However, it is actually much faster to just use the AMEX app on your phone. The number of prompts from Alexa required to accomplish anything really slows the process down. You can only make a payment when a payment is actually due, i.e., you can't pay before the due date. Not a big deal, but it's not the way I manage my account. I'll probably stick with the AMEX iPhone App instead of this skill. [16]

What's the problem here? It's that delivering actual support through a smart speaker is clunky and difficult. If you need help with a recipe, the smart speaker may be useful. If it's next to your bed and the sound of rain helps you fall asleep, it's terrific. If you want to listen to SiriusXM Satellite Radio, it's awesome. But it you want to pay your credit card bill like John T., it's a poor substitute for the online bill-pay site or the mobile app.

With the consumer excitement driving sales of smart speakers, companies like Butterball will continue to experiment with them. So let's dive a little deeper into exactly where the problems with these devices are and what it will take for them to become realistic channels through which companies and customers communicate.

Authentication is the most difficult challenge for delivering service through platforms

"I'd like to pay my bill."

"Just a second. Who are you again?"

This, in brief, is the authentication problem for technology platforms.

Skills and chatbots work better for problems where the solution is generic—the same for everyone. To make a weather forecast, Alexa needs only to know where you are located, not who you are. The Sephora chatbot on Facebook Messenger asks you questions about your skin and makes recommendations. But if you want to make changes to your account, pay a bill, move money around, upgrade your service, make a reservation—for these tasks, companies need to know *whom* they're in touch with.

It's certainly possible to authenticate yourself in these environments—but it's problematic. Authentication typically requires another device. For example, an Amazon Echo device might send a code to your phone, which you then read back to it to prove that it's actually you. But even this is not sufficient for more secure interactions. What happens if someone else comes into your house—say, your dog sitter—and then requests the Echo to provide the balance in your bank account? What if your teenage daughter asks?

This is why the most advanced banking skill on Alexa, Capital One, not only requires a login to set up but delivers only the current balance and the last five charges on a credit card. You can't pay the bill. You can't transfer money. The security required for such transactions isn't possible on Alexa. It's just easier to conduct them on your phone, where you can authenticate yourself easily with a password or fingerprint, then get the task done quickly.

Consumers are aware there's an issue. According to a 2018 consumer survey conducted by Forrester Research, 54% of US online adults worry that a voice assistant speaker will compromise the security of their private information, and 58% don't like

the idea of the device always listening in their home.[17]

It's not a coincidence that all the voice platforms prohibit skills and applications from requesting a customer's credit card. Reading your card number aloud is just too prone to problems when others could be listening. (Instead, these platforms require you to use their payment wallet systems, which is a big hurdle for most users.) Convenience and security are at odds here.

This challenge is why Bank of America elected to have its Erica chatbot run only on its mobile app—to prevent the problem of other people overhearing confidential banking transactions. As Cathy Bessant, the bank's chief technology officer, said at a 2018 Bloomberg event, "A lot of protections in a digital assistant happen at . . . the point of design. In order to use Erica, you have to take a physical action to engage Erica, a little bit like Siri. There is no potential for overhearing because the applications that support Erica can't be engaged unless there's a physical action, an authenticated action . . . to initiate the device. A lot of it has to do with [this question]: What is the mentality of the user of the AI? Our mentality is protection and confidentiality from the start."

My colleagues and I saw the same dynamic when we attempted to create a Facebook Messenger chatbot for one of America's largest retailers. The technical challenge of creating the chatbot wasn't the problem. The authentication was. The authentication actually would have required the customer to go to the retailer's site and, once there and authenticated, jump *back* into Facebook Messenger to continue the conversation.

These problems are ultimately solvable, although it may take a few years. The platforms will need to develop authentication methods and make them available to companies, much as the fingerprint readers on iPhones and Android devices are available to authenticate people using smartphone apps. Biometrics—including voice recognition—is a likely component of such authentication

methods. So yes, it's inevitable that Amazon, Google, and Facebook will provide easier ways for you to prove you're you.

But that raises another challenge. Do you trust Amazon, Google, and Facebook with your identity?

Companies don't trust conversational platforms with customers' data

Amazon, Google, and Facebook are ravenous animals when it comes to ingesting data. They succeed based on targeted advertising. The more they know, the better they target and the more they can charge for ads. These platforms are the top three companies in online ad revenues, with Google generating around $100 billion per year in ad revenue, Facebook bringing in about $34 billion, and Amazon at nearly $5 billion and growing.

The data appetites of these three platforms have created a serious impediment to companies considering building chatbots and conversational voice applications. The reason is this: these vendors refuse to promise that they won't use data from other companies' applications for their own purposes. When you're chatting with TGI Fridays on Facebook Messenger, Facebook is listening. When you're talking to Best Buy on Alexa, Amazon is listening. For retailers in particular, this is a problem, because Amazon continues to move aggressively to compete in every imaginable retail category. Why would you let a rival eavesdrop as you serve your customers?

Ty Rollin is the CTO of Mobiquity, the company that built the Butterball Alexa skill and the Nestlé application that I describe at the end of this chapter. He's got plenty of voice skills in development for other companies, but retailers in particular seem to be hanging back. "Everyone in retail is afraid of Amazon," he told me. "It is an instantaneous fright about the intelligence gathered on their business from using that voice channel. I have

some customers really, really scared about that, and it is stopping them from doing development. They are at least a year and half behind what their original plans were because of their paranoia that intelligence will be gathered about their business and used against them."

As one privacy expert I interviewed put it, "Given Amazon's overwhelming desire to own every commerce transaction, if I were a brand, I'd be concerned about creating a skill whose content could be sniffed by their servers."

Facebook has never made promises about whether it reads Facebook Messenger messages and uses the content.[18] Even if Facebook doesn't use the content of the messages for ad targeting, the platform knows which companies you are talking to. Facebook appears to be using that metadata (your location and connections), along with what brands you're looking at on their Instagram platform, to create an ad-targeting profile that works for any platform they own, including WhatsApp. Any brand—including your competitors—can use that platform to target your customers.

Facebook's new devices might be generating similar fears. Here's what its spokesperson told Recode about Facebook's new competitor to Google Home and Amazon Alexa devices, a screen-enabled product called Portal: "[D]ata about who you call and data about which apps you use on Portal *can* be used to target you with ads on other Facebook-owned properties. Portal voice calling is built on the Messenger infrastructure, so when you make a video call on Portal, we collect the same types of information (i.e., usage data such as length of calls, frequency of calls) that we collect on other Messenger-enabled devices. We may use this information to inform the ads we show you across our platforms."[19]

What about Google? Like everything else in the Google product portfolio, Google Home customizes responses based on your search history. The whole raison d'être of the Google ecosystem is combining information across applications; Google Maps shows

locations that it knows you're visiting from Google Calendar, and the assistant on your Android phone is smarter because it picks up on appointments coming in from Gmail. Google Home has had a troubled history with respect to advertising—it spontaneously promoted the live-action movie *Beauty and the Beast* in summaries of the day's events in 2017,[20] and Burger King created a TV commercial designed to get any Google Home that was listening to talk about the ingredients in a Whopper.[21] While I have no inside information about how Google plans to use, or not use, information from the applications that run on its smart speaker, it would certainly be in character for that application activity to inform the rest of the advertising that Google sells. That would include, of course, ads from the competitors of the companies that built those applications.

It's not just the companies that have privacy concerns here. Consumers are nervous, too, because they've invited these devices into their homes. As Evan Selinger, a Rochester Institute of Technology philosophy professor, told the *New York Times Magazine*, "Where are these things now appearing? They're appearing in our homes . . . The home has traditionally been the locus of privacy, right? This is where I shut out the rest of the world. This is where I look for my breathing room. This is my sanctuary, you know?"[22] Now that listening devices have invaded the sanctuary, it's just a little bit creepy.

As I speak with companies considering applications on these platforms, I hear these fears over and over. While they're intrigued about consumers' excitement about these platforms and wonder what it would take to be relevant on smart speakers or chat platforms, they don't trust the companies that run them to keep their hands off the data.

Will these platforms take over valued customer relationships?

You may imagine that your customer on Alexa is talking to you, but in fact, the customer believes she's talking to Alexa. On a website or an app, a company has the opportunity to create visual branding. But on Alexa, all too often the customer is having a conversation with the same voice that reads the weather and generates reminders.

As the CMO of one of the largest garden and home furnishing retailers told Forrester's Thomas Husson, "We clearly anticipate further disintermediation by Amazon [Alexa]."[23]

Crucially important here is what happens when bots fail. Typically, what happens on a voice platform is that when a skill or application fails, the consumer ends up talking to the platform itself, not the brand. So if you connect to the Alexa skill for Macy's and say, "Help me find cowboy boots," Macy's may give up—and you may end up talking directly to Alexa, which is happy to sell you boots on Amazon or through another vendor. Something tells me that's not what Macy's was hoping for.

When a customer service chatbot running on your site is unable to answer a question, the customer typically ends up talking to a human. If you call Avis Budget and the voice bot can't help you, it will connect your phone call to a person who can help. But you can't do that on voice platforms. When the skill or application can't figure out what you want, the response is likely to be "I'm sorry, I just don't understand." It would be great if the device connected you to a human support rep right on the smart speaker, but that capability doesn't exist yet.

And unlike apps on your phone, voice platforms have no concept of notifications. Your phone's weather app can send you an alert when a blizzard is coming, and its news app can alert you if the president is impeached. Perhaps more important, if you ask a question that takes time to figure out, the apps can message you

back when they get the answer. Alexa and Google Home devices can't—they'll just sit there. Except for the occasional alert you set up yourself ("Remind me to put the cake in the oven at 3:15"), they're completely mute—they won't even pipe up to tell you that Taylor Swift tickets are on sale.

Another big challenge is discovery. How do you find the skills you're looking for? Search is not a paradigm that works well in a voice or chat context. If I tell my smart speaker, "Start Thomson," will I end up with the financial services company, the publishing company, the travel agent, or the company that makes deck stain? (I tried this, and Alexa "helpfully" started playing songs by Richard Thompson, a 69-year-old Scottish-influenced musician I'd never heard of.) Even if you find the company you're looking for, is the bot or voice application any good? According to an analysis by Voicebot.ai, 62% of the skills on Alexa have no customer star ratings at all.[24]

Will Apple change the way companies treat platforms?

Apple is way behind in the race to create conversational platforms. Siri is less capable than Alexa or Google Assistant. So far, the capabilities of its HomePod smart speaker are quite limited (at least judging from the products that the company has released as I'm writing this in early 2019).

So why would anyone want to work with Apple?

Because unlike Facebook, Amazon, or Google, Apple doesn't sell your data or make money from advertising. In a speech to the EU's privacy commissioners in Brussels in 2018, Apple CEO Tim Cook decried the "data-industrial complex" that the rest of the tech world is creating with its advertising-driven, data-hungry tendencies. "We at Apple believe that privacy is a fundamental human right," he said. "This [the data collection by tech platforms]

is surveillance. And these stockpiles of personal data serve only to enrich the companies that collect them. This should make us very uncomfortable. It should unsettle us. And it illustrates the importance of our shared work [to preserve privacy] and the challenges still ahead of us."[25]

Apple does control a conversational platform open to companies: Apple Business Chat. (From a consumer's perspective, Apple Business Chat is what you see when you use Apple's messaging system, iMessage, to converse with companies.) And in contrast to all the other platforms, Apple has committed *not* to collect information on the content of these conversations. Basically, when a customer connects with a company on Apple Business Chat, Apple makes the connection and then gets out of the loop. You, the customer, are actually talking directly to the company, just as if you went to its website and participated in a chat there.

Apple has attracted an impressive set of early experimenters for this channel, including Burberry stores and Vodafone in Europe and Dish Network, Quicken Loans, and Mall of America in the US. These financial services, telecom, and retail companies don't have to worry about the state of data passed back and forth on iMessage, because Apple is not going to go into the banking, telecom, or retail businesses any time soon, except for selling electronics in Apple stores. Apple and its CEO believe their success will come from protecting consumers' privacy, not from collecting their data.

Apple's conversational platform is quite a bit less advanced than its competitors. But if it invests in improving Siri even as it preserves its privacy-first strategy, that could shift. From the Macintosh to the iPhone to the Apple Watch, Apple has a reputation for investing, innovating, and improving products and dominating markets with startling design and constant improvement. Apple's ability to attract partners with promises not to spy on customer interactions could generate a far more attractive set

of voice and chat applications on its platforms. It's an underdog, but if you're not watching Apple in this space, you're not seeing the whole picture.

The right strategy for maturing conversational platforms

As I've described in the first half of this book, there are compelling reasons to create virtual agents and chatbots. But those reasons all depend on delivering a better customer experience.

Even with the burgeoning popularity of messaging systems and smart speaker–type devices, you can't easily deliver a great customer experience on those platforms. Their authentication, privacy, disintermediation, and discovery problems should make you think twice.

So what should you do? Here are four recommendations.

Build virtual agents and bots on your own properties

The challenging part of conversational interfaces correctly identifying intent along with the back-end sophistication needed to address it. That's what you need to learn to do now, regardless of what's happening on Facebook's Messenger or Amazon's Alexa.

I recommend taking a page from Bank of America's book and building virtual agent or chatbot systems that work on your own site and apps. There, you'll get authentication for free, and you won't have potential conflicts with data-hungry platforms. As the conversational platforms solve their technical and partnering problems over the next few years, you'll have done the hard design work already—and you'll find that hooking your virtual agent system up to their interfaces is a lot easier than it was building them in the first place.

Build Q&A type chatbots on conversational platforms

What could you do for the customer if you *didn't* have to know who they were?

One company that embraced this strategy was Nestlé, the 150-year-old company based in Switzerland that makes everything from chocolate chips and coffee to dog food.

Nestlé has created an innovation outpost in Silicon Valley led by Josh Baillon, digital innovation manager. "Our team was created in recognition of trying to get this big company to be more agile," says Baillon. "Rather than be reactive to how things are changing, we want to be proactive about it, get ahead of the curve."

To this end, starting in 2016, Josh and his colleagues began a project to create a Nestlé presence on Amazon's Alexa.

The result was Nestlé's "GoodNes," an Alexa skill. Planning it required balancing expectation and reality. "There is a tension between the art of the technically possible and business viability," Baillon explained. Baillon and his team knew that an Alexa skill would get attention but wouldn't move the needle much on Nestlé's marketing and reputation, at least until people got far more used to talking to devices in their kitchens. Even so, he wanted to ensure that the company would have a proof-of-concept offering for home assistant devices so it could learn how best to take advantage of this new service channel.

GoodNes solves the "sticky hands" problem: cooking is messy, and sticky hands aren't a good match for laptop keyboards and tablet touchscreens. It's made up of a collection of recipes that walks home bakers through simple recipes, driven purely by voice.

Creating a skill like this is harder than it sounds. Nestlé, of course, had thousands of recipes on file. But recipes aren't designed in the kind of simple steps that voice requires. Baillon's team rapidly realized they'd need to rewrite the recipes into steps that were easy to follow and advance by voice command.

The next step was prototyping. Surprisingly, the Nestlé team

found out that this work was most effective when they tested out a script with team members role-playing two parts: the home cook and the Alexa device. The home cook would stand in the kitchen with the ingredients ready and talk to an employee who, with back turned, was playing the part of Alexa. The Alexa stand-in would respond based on the script the team had developed. This role-playing helped Nestlé's innovation team to debug the script cheaply and effectively well before spending expensive effort on coding the skill.

Once that was done, Nestlé hired Mobiquity to whip up a prototype. Six weeks later, Baillon demoed the prototype to Patrice Bula, a Nestlé executive vice president in charge of several key strategic functions, including marketing and sales. He immediately recognized that a device like this could change how people cook and agreed to unlock funding for Baillon's team to build a product that Nestlé could actually launch.

Cooking, of course, is a very visual activity. When you need to get the egg whites to the right consistency or check if the banana bread is fully cooked, you need a picture. But smart speakers don't show pictures.

Baillon's team solved that problem by creating a connection between the Alexa device and the screens in your house. To get started with GoodNes, you need to enter a first name and email address. It then sends you a link that you can open on any device with a browser: a laptop, a smartphone, or a tablet, for example. After that, as you tell your Alexa to advance to the next step in the recipe, it pushes photos and explanations to the screen you've chosen. You're talking to Alexa but viewing the process on a screen—and there's still no need to touch anything but the measuring cups and mixing bowls.

If you can design a chatbot or voice skill that answers questions that don't require authentication, it's worth the effort to get experience in conversational platforms. You can answer questions about

store hours, interest rates, stock prices, sports scores, and technical specs without knowing who's asking. If it's in your knowledge base, it can be part of your Alexa or Facebook Messenger skill. The result will be a path-bound bot, which, as I described in chapter 4, has limits. But in addition to helping your customers, it will help you get the needed experience to hook up more sophisticated bots, once the platforms work out their problems.

And if the authentication is lightweight—like the email address and customer URL that Nestlé's GoodNes skill uses to display content on a tablet, laptop, or phone—you can go a bit further. Adding a screen helps overcome some of the limitations of purely conversational interfaces.

Get a smart speaker and use it

Go buy a Google Home Hub or Amazon Alexa Echo or any of the dozens of other devices now available with smart speaker capabilities.

Then talk to them.

Ask them to wake you up at 6:30 or tell you the balance on your Capital One card or how long it will take to drive to Calgary. See how they succeed and how they fail.

Watch your family interact with them too.

There's no substitute for personal experience here. These are complicated platforms to create for, but they're simple to use. So try them out.

Closely follow developments in the conversational platform market

While most conversational platforms in 2019 are not friendly to companies, they are likely to solve their problems over the next five years or so. It won't surprise me if standards emerge that will

mitigate the concerns I've described in this chapter. To understand when it might be time to engage here, though, you'll want to carefully observe news and analyst opinions on these questions:

- Is there an easy way to authenticate users? Which platforms support it?
- Are the big platforms agreeing to act as communication channels between companies and customers, without collecting any data, as Apple Business Chat now does? Which platforms? Are those promises credible?
- Has Apple's HomePod line of products gotten any more competitive with Amazon's and Google's devices?
- Has Apple taken any steps to improve Siri's capabilities to match Alexa and Google Assistant? Has the company acquired or licensed voice and chatbot technology from other sophisticated vendors, such as Microsoft?
- What are the real capabilities of the most sophisticated apps and skills from financial services, health care, and retail companies? When you hear about a sensational skill or chat application, do the research to find out how it has solved authentication and privacy problems.

I have no doubt that the problems with these platforms will be solved, but it's tricky to predict *when*. Given their popularity, I'll be keeping close tabs on their development, and you should too.

Part III

SUCCEEDING WITH VIRTUAL AGENTS

Chapter 7

MANAGING CORPORATE RESISTANCE

What would it take to turn customer service in your company over to a machine?

This, at its base, is the question that every company exploring virtual agents faces. After all the whizzy presentations and the hype and the fear and the doubt, senior executives need to confront this question. They need to know why it will be better. They need to know why it will be cheaper. They need to come to grips with the risks and the need for acceptance from both customers and employees.

At Optus, Australia's second-largest telecom, mobile, and cable operator, this was the situation that Mark Baylis faced. Baylis had been in telecom since the 1990s and at Optus since 2006.

He believed there was enormous potential in bringing virtual agents to customer service, but now he needed to convince the company's leadership team.

The simplest approach here is a rational economic calculation. Each customer service chat agent at Optus can handle two chat sessions simultaneously. The economic objective was to reduce that cost by 50% by having virtual chat agents handle half the work. But that wouldn't be worth it unless the results were not just cheaper but better for customers. Virtual agents would have to deliver a superior customer experience and resolve issues more quickly and accurately. And they'd have to help with surges in service demand, which the company needed to manage when people got new mobile phones around Christmas and when new smartphones were launched.

From a technical standpoint, considering deploying virtual agents required rethinking what happened in customer service. Baylis had identified three key customer intents that, if automated, would have the maximum impact, plus another fifty to a hundred that were also candidates, like billing inquiries, network questions, and setting up and dealing with roaming charges on trips outside Australia. Unless the company could identify when customers were asking about these issues and deliver appropriate answers, the chatbot wouldn't have the necessary knowledge to deliver on the promise of better customer experience at lower cost.

Like all phone companies, Optus had a voice-centric culture, including voice-based call centers. But Baylis had lived through the cultural shift of introducing web chat-based customer service six years earlier, an experience that helped him navigate the technical and political challenge of introducing chatbots. "You had to find catalysts in the company that would embrace this new form of interaction and were willing to take risks and learn from them," he said. Some of the voice-based customer service managers worried that chat would create an additional channel without actually

reducing voice calls—that people would try chat, give up, and call customer service. But chat was the future.

This strategy worked—costs dropped, customer satisfaction increased, and the company has a vast collection of new data in the form of chat logs to generate insights from. Customers who got their service through chat had higher Net Promoter Scores and higher loyalty. But this new switch to virtual chat agents wasn't going to be easy, and Baylis knew they'd need to build on the original decision to implement chat as they persuaded executives to consider putting a chatbot on the other end of those chat interactions.

Finally, there was culture to deal with. Here, Baylis had a serious advantage. As he told me, "We saw a huge opportunity to transform the customer service business. This was digital transformation, a step to drive the business in a new direction." *Digital transformation* is the watchword that many companies are now focusing on to create new efficiencies and levels of service in their businesses, and Optus had committed to embrace it. A virtual agent had the potential to vastly improve the customer experience, creating a "zero human touch" conclusion. The company had already committed to that vision for its rollout of broadband nationally; the decision to deliver service through virtual agents would build on that objective.

All of these factors came into play when the system was demonstrated for the CEO, Allen Lew, and all of his direct reports in the middle of 2017. The team clearly outlined the economic, technical, and cultural arguments in favor of the rollout and demonstrated intelligent, automated chat to the executive team. And they got the green light. As one person at that meeting described, "The general reaction was excitement. It was in line with trends in the market. The leaders told us, 'This is something we must do to understand it.'"

In the wake of that meeting, Optus is now rolling out a pilot program for intelligent, automated chat agents—and planning

to implement it for voice-based service as well. It seems likely to succeed. But Mark Baylis could never have gotten there without preparing the company to make the decision on four fronts: economically, technically, politically, and culturally.

Is your company ready for virtual agents?

Every company that is considering virtual agents does so for two reasons: it provides a better customer experience, and it saves money. To make the case effectively, you must generally prove improvements on both fronts. Which you emphasize depends on what's going on strategically at your company.

But regardless of which facet of the decision you focus on, you won't succeed unless you've laid the groundwork. As Baylis learned at Optus, there are four types of questions you should ask to get that groundwork ready:

1. **Economic**—Where will you save or make money from automating your customer-facing processes?

2. **Technical**—What work will be required to get your technology infrastructure ready to connect to intelligent chatbots?

3. **Political**—What must you do to win over key executives in the company?

4. **Cultural**—What will it take for your company to become comfortable with allowing customers to interact with virtual agents as well as humans?

To get your company ready for virtual agents, you'll need to face and work through all four of these challenges.

The economic challenge: Justifying the math behind a virtual agent deployment

In the long run, putting virtual agents in place to talk to customers has the potential to improve your customer experience. But it's hard to quantify the benefit from an improvement in customer experience. As a result, you'll also need to make an economic argument for cost savings or revenue improvements.

So how do virtual agents pay for themselves?

One way is through a decrease in costs for support agents. If your company has 1,000 agents currently managing chats, those agents typically handle two chat sessions simultaneously, as they do at Optus. With virtual chat agents answering the most common questions, that ratio might shift to six chats per human agent, since a person would only need to intervene in cases where the virtual agent couldn't answer the customer's question. Do the math, and you'll see that you can get by with one-third the number of support staff—or possibly move those support staff to higher-value activities, such as upselling or training. At Dish Network, customers initiate 6 million chats per year for sales and support; letting virtual agents handle most of those requests generated tens of millions of dollars in annual savings. The company calculated that for every minute by which it could reduce the average length of time a human agent needed to spend on the phone, it could save $2 million per year.

At cable operator Charter Communications, AI-based virtual agents enabled the company to automate 50% of customer service chats. And a global event ticket retailer deploying chatbots was able to increase efficiency enough to shut down a whole contact center. While shutting down a contact center is unusual, using contact center staff with a great deal more efficiency is quite common. Because companies have to staff for times of peak volume, virtual agents' ability to directly address questions is a crucial way to keep staff costs under control.

A second way to prove the economic value of virtual agents is to pursue an increase in sales. For example, at Dish Network, one of the first places that virtual agents became useful was in the run-up to pay-per-view fights, such as boxing and mixed martial arts matches. Dish was leaving revenue unrealized because it did not have sufficient human agents to handle all the customer requests for information and orders from people signing up just before these fights aired. With intelligent virtual agents in place to handle questions about the fights, Dish was able to recognize over $6 million in pay-per-view fight revenue.

What about customer experience benefits? Virtual agents can create improvements by simplifying customers' interface with the company. In a typical company, it's not practical to have a single toll-free number on a "contact us" page, because the variety of requests is so varied. A customer might be calling to get technical support, check on an order, place a new one, or get information on any of a hundred or more products. Companies solve this problem by having multiple websites and numbers—which is hard for the consumer to navigate—or by having customers listen and respond to many options on an interactive voice response system (the dreaded "press two for printers, press three for PCs, press four to check the status of an order," and so on.) These systems drive customers crazy and prevent the company from delivering effective service.

Because virtual agents can respond to free-form text input, a company can often put a single chat interface in front of multiple technical and support systems. If the customer enters the chat and types, "I want to find out if my order shipped," the system knows to connect to the order tracking system. If instead the customer types, "My printer refuses to recognize the ink cartridge," the chatbot recognizes the request as a support question. In this way, a chat interface can increase the number of successfully resolved requests by simplifying the way customers get in contact with the company. Like the Google search box, you can

enter many different questions into the chat box, regardless of format, and get an answer.

Forrester Research analysts Daniel Hong and Ian Jacobs, in a report called *Unlock The Hidden Value of Chatbots For Your Customer Service Strategy*, suggest looking beyond cost reduction for additional benefits.[1] These benefits include the ability to hoover up and review customer data; improving experiences, especially for impatient millennial customers; and enabling new customer service models. Once virtual agents are in place, you'll be able to gain new insights into what's really happening in your customer service environments. (For example, one gaming company figured out that 4% of its total chat traffic was fraudulent phishing attempts.)

The technical challenge: Is your infrastructure ready?

Even if you can justify the decision through cost savings or customer experience improvements, you may not be ready to put virtual agents in place. If your corporate systems are not appropriately prepared and configured, your project is not likely to succeed. Here are six things to check about your technology:

1. **Do APIs exist (or can you build them) to connect to all key systems?** Every request to a virtual agent eventually results in a query to a corporate system. That system might be a subscriber system, one that keeps track of orders, or one that holds technical support questions. For example, at a cable operator, there is a system that determines what TV channels a subscriber is supposed to have access to and whether he's paid his bill; another that determines if the network is having problems in a geographical area; and another that keeps track of what support requests the subscriber has had in the past. A virtual agent must have access

to all of those systems to get quick answers to questions like "Is this subscriber supposed to be able to see HBO, and what might be getting in the way?" APIs allow these computer systems connect with each other and to virtual agent systems. Until the APIs on a company's key systems are in place and working dependably, there's no practical way to connect a virtual agent to those systems. (For more detail on how corporate information architecture is crucial to your readiness for virtual agents, see the next chapter.)

2. **Are the systems working with subsecond response times?** Customers are impatient with computer systems in a way they aren't with humans. Computer responses must come back in milliseconds; a response that takes more than one second is going to cause a problem. While a human in such an interaction can realistically explain the problem ("I'm waiting for the customer system to respond; if you can be patient for a moment, I know we'll get the information we're looking for"), a virtual agent typically can't. For this reason, any company that wants to connect chatbots needs not just API connections but connections that respond quickly.

3. **Are the systems extremely reliable?** If a system is up and working properly only 95% of the time, then an unacceptable 50 out of every 1,000 calls will end up dissatisfied. An automated system can't apologize sincerely, offer discounts to make up for service problems based on judgment, or deal gracefully with customer profanity and sarcasm. For this reason, the APIs and the systems they connect to must be up and working 99.9% of the time, or even more if the call volume is large enough.

4. **Can the systems scale effectively?** The test of a virtual agent system is how it handles surges of traffic. Consider the situation of a retailer, for example: What happens on the few days before the Christmas holiday when call volume is at a maximum? For an electronics product that requires a complex setup, what happens on Christmas day as people open their presents? For an airline, what happens when thousands of reservations are cancelled because of a line of thunderstorms or a volcanic eruption, like the one in Eyjafjallajökull, Iceland, that crippled European air travel in 2010? (Recognize that in the absence of virtual agents, customers in these situations would typically have to spend long hours waiting on the phone to get any service at all.)

5. **Can the most costly questions be automated?** Chatbots will always need to turn questions over to human agents when those questions are special and unexpected cases. For example, at a telecom operator, "My phone won't connect to the network" is a common question. "A llama ate my phone" is not. Typically, the top set of intents cover 90% of the traffic; if you can automate those, then the virtual agent deployment is likely to be effective. As I mentioned in chapter 2, defining the list of types of intents is crucial to determining if a chatbot can respond to those intents.

6. **Is the necessary data available?** You can't get started with a virtual agent project unless there's a pool of data to analyze to identify the intents that matter to customers. As artificial intelligence expert Seth Earley says, "Organizations that want to use this technology will have to collect the right data to understand their customers' journeys." The availability of that data can make or break an AI project. (I discuss data readiness in more detail in the next chapter.)

The political challenge: Winning over executives

Who owns the decision to deploy virtual agents? At most companies, this is a complicated question.

As you may recall from the story about Avis Budget in chapter 1, the most powerful impetus typically comes from the person responsible for the business that the virtual agents will affect. At Avis Budget in Europe, that business owner was the EVP in charge of the call center. Such business owners are typically reaching a point of frustration because the cost, speed, or accuracy of people-intensive systems are preventing the business from moving forward.

But while line-of-business owners may become excited about the possibilities of chatbots cutting costs, other executives may be more interested in the impact—positive or negative—on the customer's experience. For example, Dish Network has a corporate goal to be tops in the J. D. Power customer service rankings. So the decision about virtual agents there closely connected with questions about how it would affect customer satisfaction.

Still other executives will become involved because the engineering for virtual agents requires changes to their systems.

In a typical virtual agent decision, in addition to the business owner, these executives will usually be involved:

- The CIO and some of his or her direct reports, because the chatbots must connect to so many corporate systems;
- The head of support and sometimes the head of sales, because the system will have dramatic effects on support structures, methods, and costs;
- The chief experience officer, the head of customer experience, or whatever other executive is responsible for the

customer journeys and overall customer experience for the company;

- The COO, who is ultimately responsible for the way the business runs; and

- Other executives, such as the head of product management, the CMO, or the head of human resources, because the chatbot decision may impact the company's brand or its staff.

Unless multiple executives are allied behind the decision, it's unlikely to get off the ground.

With so many executives involved, there are many potential people who can say no. For example, if the information systems to which the virtual agents will connect are in the midst of transition, that transition will probably have to be completed before it's possible to deploy the virtual agents. If the company's HR processes have resulted in embarrassing incidents in the past, then a change that would result in reassigning many staff might be politically difficult.

On the other hand, some initiatives can unify the political process. Many companies, including Optus, are in the midst of a digital transformation that combines and connects systems to deliver better and more efficient services to customers. Virtual agents are a natural part of such a transformation.

The same would apply if the company is in a situation where cost cutting has become a priority. Similarly, if customer experience has become central to the company's strategy, properly designed virtual agents can help create a more consistent and satisfactory experience.

Executives investigating the possibility of putting virtual agents in place must review corporate priorities, identify those

that support the decision, and then win over executives based on those priorities.

The cultural challenge: Will attitudes and business rules get in the way?

Even if you've cleared the political, economic, and political hurdles to deploying virtual agents, you may still face cultural hurdles. In many cases, those hurdles are the most challenging to overcome.

The main cultural hurdle is prejudice: the belief that human agents can always deliver a better customer experience than virtual ones. This may be a hidden assumption at your company, especially among the people who manage those support representatives.

The reality, of course, is that consumers would often prefer to interact with a machine rather than a human—if that machine can get to the answer quickly. This is why the web took off in the '90s and apps became successful in the past decade. Consumers preferred clicking on their computers or tapping on their phones to see when a package would arrive or what their bank balance was—the result was quicker and more dependable.

Now consumers, especially young consumers, have become frustrated with talking on the phone. According to a 2016 survey from Open Market, given the choice, 75% of millennials would choose texting over talking on the phone.[2] Voice minutes are declining; for example, in the UK, total minutes spent on voice calls dropped 15% between 2010 and 2015.[3] In 2013, Vodafone said the average length of calls on its network had dropped by half in the previous five years.[4]

Just as consumers became comfortable with websites and apps, they will become happier with chatbots—provided the chatbots can actually answer most of the questions. When making the case, executives need to see how virtual agents can turn customers

over to human agents when the virtual agent can't identify the problem—and also what percentage of chats the virtual agents can handle and how they affect customer satisfaction. To answer all of these questions, it pays to begin with a pilot project that you believe will have a high chance of success, both in improving customer experience and reducing costs. This is what it takes to win over biased folks at the company.

Business rules which reflect cultural bias can also thwart chatbot projects

Sometimes a company has the will, but the rules get in the way. Rules may require a human agent in the loop where a sale is at risk, a customer is ready to defect, or fraud is possible. The reasoning is this: a person can make the emotional connection and exercise judgment in a way a virtual agent cannot. Sometimes this makes sense; sometimes it doesn't.

For example, one international credit card company I work with has a set of business rules specifying that if you file a claim to challenge fraudulent charges, you must talk to a person before the claim can go through. This is because the company was concerned that if a machine were on the other end, those filing claims might figure out a way to game the system.

Whatever rules may be getting in the way of deployment, the key in these situations is to take a step back and ask if the cultural reasons behind the rules make sense. Once a virtual agent is part of the experience, it often turns out that you can apply the rules differently and have a successful outcome.

For example, at SiriusXM, the original rule specified that if you used the chat interface and said you wanted to cancel your subscription, you'd have to talk to a human chat agent. There were good reasons for this: chat agents could use their judgment to offer appropriate discounts or packages to attempt to retain

customers who wanted to cancel. But a closer look at the data revealed that half of the people who were cancelling were doing so simply because they had sold their old car (along with its radio) and were getting a new one. When they said they wanted to cancel, they often meant "cancel and set up a subscription on a new car." A simple tweak to the virtual agent interface—asking "Have you just sold your car?"—made it possible for virtual agents to handle these switchovers and relieved the human agents from another straightforward, automatable task.

A final cultural obstacle: The omnipotent IT team

There's one more reason that companies never get around to implementing chatbots. It's that they think they can do it themselves.

As I discussed earlier in the book, it's certainly easy to set up a simple rule-based chatbot that can answer a limited set of questions. But that kind of chatbot won't succeed in customer service or sales situations.

Another approach is to turn the chatbot project over to the cleverest data scientists in the IT department. That rarely works.

A typical virtual agent project involves API engineering, customer journey analysis, natural language processing, and machine learning. It requires a system that can balance loads that shift over time and turn calls or chats over gracefully to human agents when required. These are specialized skills most IT teams won't have in house. But if they imagine they do, they may embark on a project. You may still be waiting to see results three years later.

Ironically, such projects are often solving problems that other companies have already solved. A credit card company's virtual agents probably ought to operate similarly to the virtual agents from another credit card company; an airline chatbot is going to be similar to one from another airline. That's why it typically makes

sense to outsource the virtual agent engineering to a company that's already built similar interfaces for other companies.

Prepare well and start slow

Even if you've made the economic case, prepped the technology, wrangled the politics, and revealed and dealt with the cultural issues, your best chance of success remains moving slowly toward virtual agent implementation. This is why Dish Network first tested intelligent chat in sales with customers who wanted to sign up for pay-per-view fights and why Optus is testing its own program with a limited rollout.

A rollout in a single region or with a single product or limited percentage of customers makes sense. Things go wrong. You'll need time to identify and solve problems. And you'll need time for those executives who are still uncomfortable with the rollout to get used to it.

As I've seen with our clients SiriusXM and Dish Network, among others, a limited rollout also allows the people working on the system to identify and fine-tune the metrics they'll use to show the implementation is working. It also allows you to prove to senior executives that the system is working with real customers, which helps reassure everyone that it's ready for a broader rollout.

You may find, as both Optus and Dish did, that the limited rollout creates an appetite for more. You may find executives who were virtual agent opponents stealthily angling to get their departments set up next. You'll be on your way to rolling things out more broadly, getting more buy-in, aligning your system with more intents, and imagining new ways to turn virtual agents into a better experience for your customers.

To go much further, though, you'll have to consider the architecture of your customer systems. That takes a new way of thinking about IT. And it's the topic of the next chapter.

Chapter 8

THE ARCHITECTURE OF THE FUTURE

There was once a major online retailer that decided to implement virtual agents. I won't reveal the name of company for reasons that will soon become clear, but what you are about to read actually happened.

This online retailer worked with millions of customers as well as large numbers of suppliers. The cost for its support calls continued to grow. But a careful analysis of the calls showed that the number of identifiable intents for those callers was manageable—in the range of about 60 or 70. Many of those intents could be recognized and automated. For example, when a supplier called to request an increase in credit limit, a human support person made that decision. If the virtual agent system could identify that intent, it could apply the company's rules and make a decision about whether to approve the request or not.

The goal of the project leader at this retailer, let's call him Steven, was modest. Steven wanted to automate at least 10% of the support requests, reducing the demands on the human support agents. If the system could identify most of the intents, that goal was well within reach.

In working with him, we did what we always do in these situations. We trained the system on a large corpus of information from past chats. We were successful at recognizing the intent of a support request about three-quarters of the time.

Having recognized the intent, the system then passed the intent on to a "decisioning engine" within the retailer. This component looked at the characteristics of the person requesting support and returned a decision about what to do.

The decisioning engine was highly consistent. Over 95% of the time, it returned the same answer: "Transfer to agent."

They should have called it an "indecisioning engine."

Steven, the project leader, didn't give up easily. He identified the source of the complexity, which included the way that the decisioning engine took into account many different variables including the caller's geography and history with the company. He talked to senior executives at the company who were involved with the decisioning engine to attempt to get permission to improve it. He reached out to four different people at the company who, collectively, were directly responsible for the decisioning engine.

But nobody was willing to make a change. No one wanted to touch it.

Over time, the code in the decisioning engine had become so intricate and interdependent that everyone was afraid to make the slightest change. It remained a glowing, active component at the heart of the system, completely opaque and impervious to improvement.

In the end, the effort spent creating a virtual agent system at this retailer was a complete waste. As long as the ineffective

decisioning engine remained an essential part of the process, no useful automation was possible.

And as far as I know, the company is continuing with the same inflexible, inefficient system and the same dependence on support reps that it had when it started this effort.

As virtual agents become part of support systems everywhere, this retailer will remain a laggard. That's got nothing to do with the viability of virtual agents, recognizing intents, or customers' or suppliers' attitudes toward working with machines. It's a simple matter of an architecture so inflexible that progress is impossible.

Systems of record and systems of engagement

The problem at this online retailer is hardly unique. Problems like this have been happening for years and years. Here's a way to think about it.

In 2011, the legendary technology thinker Geoffrey Moore, author of *Crossing the Chasm*, wrote a seminal paper called "Systems of Engagement and The Future of Enterprise IT" for the AIIM, the Association for Intelligent Information Management. In the paper, he drew a distinction between two types of information systems at the heart of every company: systems of record and systems of engagement.

As Moore's paper described, systems of record included the massive, secure, and bulletproof systems that businesses depend on, such as reservation systems, customer databases, and resource provisioning systems. These systems were dependable, but they were slow and difficult to change. They often ran on large traditional servers rather than in modern, flexible environments in the internet cloud.

Companies also built systems of engagement to connect with customers who needed to move faster than the stodgy systems

of record. When you think of systems of engagement, think of websites with reservation forms or online catalogues, for example. These systems were open to regular customers, not just the high priests of information technology within a company. Plus, they had to process consumers' actions quickly.

As Moore wrote about the rise of systems of engagement, "What is transpiring is momentous, nothing less than the planet wiring itself a new nervous system. If your organization is not linked into this nervous system, you will be hard pressed to participate in the planet's future. . . . [I]f you expect these folks [digital natives] to be your customers, your employees, and your citizens (and, frankly, where else could you look?), then you need to apply THEIR expectations to the next generation of enterprise IT systems. But of far more immediate importance is how much productivity gains businesses and governments are leaving on the table by not following the next generation's lead."

But the systems of record are not going anywhere. They remain at the heart of every company. The challenge is, as it was for the online retailer with the indecisioning engine, to connect those legacy systems to the systems of engagement that now function as the visible face of the company for customers who want to interact with it.

My cowriter, Josh Bernoff, wrote about this in his 2013 book, *The Mobile Mind Shift*. That book concerned the challenges of connecting rigid systems of record to impatient customers on mobile devices. (Think of a customer requesting a boarding pass from an American Airlines app or trying to determine if she has enough money in the bank to make a debit card purchase; in both cases, a highly responsive app must communicate with systems of record within the airline or the bank.) As Josh and his coauthors on that book, Ted Schadler and Julie Ask, wrote:

> For 30 years, companies have been building the technology systems to power PCs on employees' desks and then websites on customers' PCs. They built software to connect tools to the big corporate systems of record that manage things like inventory and customer records. The result of all this activity, in most large companies, is technological chaos of complexity, redundancy, and antiquity . . .
>
> Your complex systems aren't designed to deliver simple mobile experiences. These systems were built for employees sitting at desks all day tending complex processes, not for casual customers taking action in seconds on a mobile device.

More than five years have passed since that was published, but the problem remains the same. The only difference is that instead of "mobile," you could write "chatbot."

These challenges played out with the rise of the web. They played out again with mobile apps. Now that the focus of interactivity is shifting to chat and voice conversations, the historical tension between rigid systems of record and agile systems of engagement is playing out once again.

Virtual agents are the center of this desire to connect systems because they have the unique ability to connect to, draw intelligence from, and interact with multiple systems at the speed that engaged customers demand. Furthermore, they can power interactions across multiple channels—voice, chat, conversational platforms like Alexa, even SMS text messaging.

In a Medium article called "The New Moats," Jerry Chen of Greylock Partners invented the idea of systems of intelligence. A system of intelligence creates value by spanning the systems of record and the systems of engagement. As Chen wrote, "What

makes a system of intelligence valuable is that it typically crosses multiple data sets, multiple systems of record."[1] And he believes such systems are key to creating defensible business for the future that will be hard to disrupt.

As I'll describe in this chapter, virtual agents are the systems of intelligence that Chen described. They are the catalyst you need to finally get your systems of record ready to deliver at the speed of systems of engagement.

So long as customer systems of record remain rigid and inflexible, progress on new forms of interaction will be challenging. But change becomes possible with the right kind of motivation. That's what happened at a large hotel chain, where I saw a story that started just like the online retailer's—but ended up very differently.

How a hotel chain unlocked access to its own systems

Executives at a major hotel chain hoped to transform their customer service operation. Customer service costs were cutting into profit—especially for calls with no revenue associated with them, such as calls to cancel reservations. So the company began working to automate those service calls through virtual agents.

Just as at the retailer, progress stalled. The first problem was helping provide customer service interfaces to multiple corporate systems. Connecting and rationalizing those systems would require IT staff to free up budget to code interfaces—APIs—to those systems. The response from these various technology teams was consistently to say something along the lines of, "I can't give you access to my system. I can't share that data."

And second, there was the problem of authentication. While some intents, such as finding an appropriate hotel, did not require authentication, others, such as checking the points balance in a loyalty program, did. The hotel chain had to make sure no one

could call up and cancel somebody else's reservation, transfer points that didn't belong to them, or reset someone else's password.

Both of the problems ran afoul of a broader question: security. The information security staff at the chain were reluctant to make changes, since they were incented to keep the systems secure and prevent breaches, not to open those systems up to new forms of interaction like a bot, even though these new forms of interactions would benefit the hotel chain by reducing cost and improving the customer experience.

But the will to change things at this hotel chain was strong, and the corporate leadership and technology executives were unwilling to remain saddled with the shortcomings in their systems of record.

The solutions to these problems happened at two levels: the executive level and the technology level.

The executive meeting kicked off with a fair-sized group, 12 people in all, including the CIO and several of his senior vice presidents. They heard from people involved with generating revenue, including the chief revenue officer and the senior executive in charge of customer experience. The technology leaders learned that management had committed to significant cost savings from the project and were willing to invest in technology spending to deliver on those promises.

Thirty-five people responsible for various parts of the hotel chain's systems assembled for a more detail-oriented technology meeting to figure out how to execute on the charge from management.

They learned best practices for authentication and eventually figured out that they could have the virtual agent system use the same verification methods that the human agents were using—rewards numbers, last hotel stayed at, or home address, for example.

Finally, and most importantly, they learned what each other's constraints and obstacles were and figured out how they could

work together toward solutions. They developed a common goal—automating and speeding up the customer service system, improving the experience and saving cost—and created a plan to work toward it.

The hotel chain has now been connecting systems and building APIs for about a year. This was necessary work that would have eventually been done anyway, but the virtual agent project moved it to the top of the priority list. The hotel chain's interactive voice response system is about to be replaced with voice bots, and no one will miss it less than the customers will. As I write this, the chain plans to put virtual agents in both channels, phone and chat, and to deliver a better experience at lower cost, just as they committed to do a year ago.

Flexibility must be the new goal of technology

The goal of corporate technology has always been to be rock solid. The focus was on reliability, not on change. That was appropriate for a world where consumers expected the same thing each year as they had the year before.

But waves of consumer technology—and the expectations that go along with them—keep changing. Consider banking. When ATMs came along and you didn't have to go the teller to cash a check, that was a huge deal. When apps allowed you to check your balance, that was even better. When you could deposit checks by taking a picture, that raised expectations again. Now, as I described in chapter 3, Bank of America has a chatbot that you ask to solve your problems.

The goal of technology now is not only to be secure and dependable but to flex to adjust to the new demands that are placed on it.

Flexibility wins. Consider Tom Brady, the quarterback of the New England Patriots. He continues to deliver passes on target to receivers—and to get up, ready to go, after being pounced on

by defenders—even though, as I write this, he's 41 years old. He's two years older than any other starting quarterback playing in 2018, and he intends to continue playing for years, while other quarterbacks who entered the league in the same year he did are long retired. How is this possible? It's because while the rest of the league was training for strength, he was training for pliability and flexibility. A strong quarterback might be able to stay standing half a second longer in the grip of a defender, but a flexible one can twist out of the way—and can remain a viable contributor for years longer.

In the same way, your corporate technology systems in 2018 must be engineered for flexibility, not just for dependability. As Jessica Groopman, industry analyst and founding partner at the research firm Kaleido Insights, wrote in her 2018 report *AI Readiness: Five Areas Businesses Must Prepare for Success in Artificial Intelligence*:[2]

> [A] variety of companies we interviewed—both suppliers and adopters of machine learning—suggest building for flexibility. This takes a number of forms, for example:
>
> - Emphasize ease of spinning new services up and down
> - Don't just allow for integrations, build this into strategy and product roadmap
> - Differentiate by providing integration capabilities at the app layer or in configuration efficiency, instead of deeper in the stack
> - Focus on user-facing app development so as to expedite tighter feedback loops among outputs, interactions, and the enterprise.

Groopman's team interviewed 27 companies and AI experts for her report. Here's how she sums up their attitudes: "Companies [we] interviewed reinforce the importance of thinking about AI as cyclical or evolving, not linear or defined by a single destination. This isn't just about the performance of a model, but should also be informed by new data sources, APIs, integrations, regulations, techniques, security reconfigurations, and cultural changes."

This won't be easy. Traditional relational databases and other systems of record aren't designed for the loads and levels of responsiveness that AI demands. As Google researchers described in a 2015 study,[3] AI and machine-learning systems exacerbate technical debt, the challenge of maintaining old code to keep it aligned with new priorities. But the costs of failing to update technical infrastructure can be even worse—an inability to respond to competitive pressures.

If you don't have a flexible architecture and the ability to move fast, you're not going to be able to keep up to date. A hotel chain might have to start listing private homes to compete with Airbnb. A bank may need to generate new credit card numbers on the fly. A car rental company may need to be ready to deliver self-driving cars, some of which might belong not to the company but to private individuals who aren't using them right now. A media company may need to start selling and provisioning streams rather than delivering programs to distributors. And all of those organizations may have to deliver those capabilities through mobile apps, chatbots, Alexa queries, and who knows what interface in the future—maybe eye blinks in virtual reality headsets. The point is not to predict what's coming and when, which is difficult. It's to have systems that are ready to flex in the direction of those changes as soon as the changes come along.

In the rest of this chapter, I describe what goals and principles you should have in mind as you work on improving your technology infrastructure to build in flexibility.

Improved customer experience is the key motivator

Gianni Giacomelli is a leading AI thinker and the chief innovation officer at Genpact, a GE spinoff that helps companies build AI applications. I like what he told Kaleido Insights about AI readiness: "No matter which lens you're [using to assess] readiness—of data, of infrastructure, of employees—the ultimate question must always be, How will this impact the end-to-end customer experience?"

As you consider investments in improving the architecture of your systems, this is the question that should be foremost in your mind.

Will the changes you're planning get people the answers they seek about your products or services?

Will they deliver those answers more quickly and in more communication channels?

Will they allow people to make and modify their orders with the company with less hassle?

As I described in chapter 1, the best current business research now shows that companies that make improvements in customer experience are more likely to see growth and profit than other companies. But every company wants to give customers what they want with less friction. What gets in the way?

Inflexible architecture and systems that don't connect. Anyone who's ever had a customer service rep tell them "I can't make the change you requested" or "I can't see that information" knows what I mean.

Fix your architecture, and you'll be closer to delivering on that customer experience goal. The improvements in infrastructure that matter will reduce costs without any impact on Net Promoter Scores or customer satisfaction—and, ideally, will improve them.

Especially now, a greater proportion of customers, especially younger customers, expect your digital systems to deliver whatever

they want in their preferred digital channels, whether that's chat, Facebook, Siri, apps, or by phone. If your architecture prevents that, they'll see you as lame . . . and they'll kick you to the curb in favor of suppliers who can give them what they want.

Better data is the fuel that flexible architecture runs on

If your data is flawed, poorly structured, or not consistently accessible, your systems will fail. You can't set up a virtual agent properly unless it can get good answers to questions about the customers using it: what have they done in the past, how many times have they contacted the company, what are their preferences?

As AI expert Seth Earley wrote, "AI is applied human knowledge. Organizations need to develop the foundations for advancing AI by capturing and curating that knowledge and by building the foundational data structures that form the scaffolding for that knowledge. . . . [T]ruly personalizing the user experience requires that product data be correctly structured and organized, that content processes be integrated into product onboarding, and that associations can be made among products, content, and user intent signals."[4]

Bad data is an obstacle. Kaleido Insights' Groopman explained it to me this way: "No data, no AI. Data—and even more importantly, *good* data—is the prerequisite to any machine learning. You have to get the ingredients in order, but that is easier said than done. Sourcing, assembling, cleaning, and preparing the right data consumes around 80% of the time that data scientists spend these days. You can't actualize data science until you have basic needs in place; for AI, data preparedness is as basic as food, shelter, or water."

Regulated industries like financial services and health care already spend a lot of energy on data hygiene—because if they don't, they get fined. But this should be a best practice for any

company now. Before hooking up systems, conduct an audit of data quality. Identify processes that are creating or perpetuating the spread of bad data. Invest in fixing these processes before you hook up a bot.

Human agents can try to use judgment to correct for bad data (although it often causes them to make mistakes that aren't really their fault). But virtual agents consuming bad, questionable, incomplete, or inconsistent data will fail.

Don't automate stupid processes

Data quality and systems aren't the only sources of chaos in the journey toward flexible architecture. Poor processes also create challenges.

Not all processes ought to be automated. Some ought to be scrapped. As Greg Spratto, creator of a successful internal chatbot system at Autodesk, puts it, "You don't want to automate processes that were crappy to begin with. Good candidates for automation can sometimes be good candidates for policy change." So if your processes involve management approval for trivial matters or require sending requests and getting returns back days later, then virtual agents won't make the process any better.

An American friend of mine recently saw an example of this when he caused minor damage to his rental car during a European trip. His credit card was supposed to cover the damage. But getting the problem resolved took four months of back and forth between the driver, the Dutch rental car company, the US credit card company, and the insurance firm that the credit card company had outsourced the problems and resolutions to. This was a process that could take place only partially online but also required the driver to manage connections between the rental car company and the other parties, including phone calls to harass them until some action happened. It's a perfect example of a twisted and complex

process that delivers a poor customer experience. Virtual agents couldn't improve it because it's screwed up to begin with.

Avoid the fantasy of the 360-degree customer view

Why stop with APIs and access? Why not go all the way to integrating every customer system the company has?

This is the myth of the 360-degree view of the customer. It's a dangerous fantasy that's out of touch with the way real information systems work within companies.

According to one survey conducted by a renowned technology research company, fewer than 10% of large companies have a 360-degree view of customers. In my opinion, even the few people who said they have one are deluded. The number of customer interactions is expanding massively, as customers tap on mobile apps, visit websites, and interact with sales and customer care representatives. I've actually seen a purported "360-degree view" system—it was at a cable operator. They'd spent over $80 million on the system. It was filled with massive amounts of data about customers—not just when they had service calls but what they viewed on their set-top boxes. And it was useless. It included so much information that it became impossible to see what was important.

Marketing experts Nick Worth and Dave Frankland have observed the pernicious appeal of this fantasy in their 2018 book *Marketing to the Entitled Consumer.* They write, "Again and again, we've seen companies fail as they attempt to overhaul all their systems to create what they hope will be a 360-degree view of the customer. That's an effort that could cost hundreds of millions of dollars, take years to implement, and end up obsolete as soon as it's completed, as customers and companies develop new ways of interacting."

As one analyst told us, universal solutions like this soak up

the budget and energy that ought to be going into more practical projects. He cited the fantasy of "one chatbot to rule them all." You're far better off improving architectures and solving a particular set of problems, such as customer service or sales issues or credit approvals. Because if you wait for the 360-degree view of the customer to be complete—or try to design a chatbot that solves all problems—you'll never live to see any practical benefits.

You need a plan to improve your architectural flexibility

APIs and other connections are the key here—building them is going to be a big part of what IT departments do in the future, because that's what's needed for flexibility. At some companies I've worked with, mergers and acquisitions from a decade ago are still visible in the form of incompatible customer systems. Systems that were set up to deliver data with overnight "batch processing models" need updates to provide interactive feeds to mobile and AI applications. Some depend on third-party vendors, like SABRE in the airline industry.

Could robotic process automation (RPA), the technology that I described in chapter 5, solve these problems? RPA can quickly connect systems together without code, and for that reason, it's a great way to connect systems of record that, until now, could only be accessed by humans logging into them and typing or clicking. But RPA is not a long-term architectural solution. RPA is brittle—changes in the underlying software or operating systems can cause it to stop working until an IT staffer figures out where the connections broke down and fixes it again. RPA is a decent way to get things going. But in the long term, the flexible connections of APIs are the only way to create an architecture in which the systems of record and the systems of engagement keep working together effectively.

The companies that succeed in building flexible architecture have a plan. For every short-term fix they create, such as a new customer database to launch a new product, they have a long-term plan to bring systems together and modernize architecture with more open, cloud-based information systems.

For example, at more advanced banks and credit card companies, the decisioning systems are not black boxes like the one in the story of the internet retailer that started this chapter. They can look at a customer's history of, for example, paying bills on time and reflect that by making quick decisions on disputed charges. One travel company I worked with moved all its reservations to a Salesforce database within a year and half after a merger. Systems integrators such as Accenture, Infosys, and Cognizant have the skills to make these migrations work. Every company has imperfect information systems. You might see this as an obstacle to the implementation of virtual agents that interact with those systems. But my experience, and the experience of my company, has been the complete opposite. Virtual agents can create the impetus to provide the necessary connections to corporate systems and modernize them when it is difficult to get budget for them in any other way. Your customer service agents are already functioning as "virtual APIs," integrating the information from corporate systems at high cost with a great deal of inefficiency and inconsistency. Instead of maintaining this flawed status quo, you can use virtual agents as a catalyst for change; the companies that make that change are able to move more quickly as other technology needs arise in the future. This is a far more productive attitude than rallying to defend a broken system, like the internet retailer's indecisioning engine, that anchors the company's infrastructure to obsolescence.

Virtual agents have the unique ability to bridge multiple systems and respond quickly. They can now do what previously only people could do—albeit slowly and inconsistently—which

is to combine data from multiple sources and make a judgment. All that's needed is to make the necessary connections available.

So assess the state of your systems with the help of your IT and development pros. Find high-level support and reasons to move forward—like the promised cost savings from a merger or an ability to catch up to or surpass nimbler competitors. Make the investments you need to build a flexible architecture, not just for connections to virtual agents but to prepare yourself for the systems of engagement of the future.

Digital transformation is the ultimate goal

Somewhere just past the goal of a more flexible architecture is a more profound objective: digital transformation. This is not a pie-in-the-sky vision like the 360-degree customer view. Instead it's an evolution of the company and its systems toward the long-term realization that all business is about to be digital.

What is digital transformation? George Westerman, principal research scientist with the MIT Sloan Initiative on the Digital Economy, described it as "a radical rethinking of how an enterprise uses technology to radically change performance."[5] Forrester's Nigel Fenwick and Ted Schadler, in their report *Digital Rewrites The Rules Of Business*, described the objective of digital transformation this way: "Harness digital assets and ecosystems to continually improve customer outcomes and, simultaneously, increase operational effectiveness."[6] Their view of the future looks like this:

> By 2022, your artificial intelligence and machine-learning systems will be handling or supporting the vast majority of your customer interactions. These systems will be highly attuned to each customer's preferences and able to tailor each engagement based on

> your customer's context and moment of need. Your customers will rapidly come to expect this level of tailored service. They won't tolerate employees not anticipating their needs.

Something fundamental is going on here. For example, as the *New York Times* pondered its digital future, its best forward-looking thinkers wrote, "While the past two years have been a time of significant innovation, the pace must accelerate. Too often, digital progress has been accomplished through workarounds; now we must tear apart the barriers."[7]

What does this kind of thinking actually mean? It's simple to describe and hard to do.

It's working toward a state where all manual and paper-based processes are replaced with digital processes.

It requires rethinking processes around improvements in customer experience and then reworking those processes to remove clumsy, old-fashioned, or politically driven manual processes.

It means operations that are fully measurable and instrumented, giving unprecedented insight into which strategies and parts of the company are successful and which need rethinking.

It's about speed. Once a company's architecture begins to shift in a fully digital direction, it's easier to flex. It's easier for companies to protect themselves from disruptive upstarts. It becomes possible to rethink business models and develop new products or tap in to new sets of customers.

Digital transformation is a long-term goal and a worthwhile one. It's hard to imagine any successful company in ten years that will not be fully digital and leveraging AI in all parts of its business.

The flexible architecture I've described in this chapter is a crucial milestone as a company pursues digital transformation. It's not just about making systems ready for virtual agents. It's

about making companies ready for a revolution driven by virtual and AI technologies of all kinds.

While it's difficult to see clearly what that future might be, it's not at all difficult to understand what it will take to get there. Investments in flexible systems are crucial. That's why you need to start planning them now.

Chapter 9

THE POWER OF CUSTOMER JOURNEY ANALYTICS

Lori Bieda is passionate about two things. One is customer experience. The other is analytics: the science of using data to generate powerful insights.

Bieda has been studying analytics for 25 years, with a heavy focus on the financial sector across the US, Canada, and Latin America. For the past three years, she's led the Data and Analytics Centre of Excellence at Bank of Montreal (BMO), one of the ten largest banks in North America. She didn't start as a math geek, but the more she sought for the truth about what mattered

to customers and to the companies she worked for, the more she recognized that that truth was hiding in the data the company collected, waiting for the right analytical approach.

What approach is that? It's an approach rooted in the massive amounts of data about customers: what they click on, when they call the call center or visit a branch, what they're trying to do and how the design of the systems that the bank uses either helps or frustrates them. In the lexicon of customer experience, the paths that customers take to attempt to accomplish their goals are called "customer journeys." The science of applying data to get insights about those journeys, across all channels and all customers, is the discipline of customer journey analytics, or CJA. Data analysis, as applied to that massive data set about customers, has now become so sophisticated that it pays great dividends in customer insight.

Bieda likened the CJA approach to studying how water flows. "We create pathways for customers to go down, and they move down them like water," she explained. These journeys apply to tasks like opening a new account or paying a bill. The company's preferred journey—the series of steps that the company has designed—is like a dam that directs customer flow in the desired direction.

The problem is when the water doesn't all flow where the dam directs it. Places that you hadn't anticipated tend to get wet. What happens when lots of customers click on a dead link? The people who get caught in eddies and backwaters because they've made a mistake, or represent a special case—what happens to them? Do they turn against the bank and leave forever? Or can the bank identify the nonstandard paths they are taking and rescue them, retaining them as loyal customers?

CJA tools help analyze those anomalous paths that the bank didn't intend for customers to take, paths that typically result in customers having a poor experience.

For example, imagine that you're about to buy a new house. The bank can anticipate that you might be checking out new

neighborhoods and shifting money around. You might also be generating more bills than usual—to pay real estate lawyers and home inspectors, for example, or to buy new furniture. If, in the midst of that experience, you happen to have a problem with your online password, you'll be tossed into the bank's usual password recovery flow—not necessarily the best experience.

Passwords and mortgages are completely different parts of the bank's experience design. But at BMO, CJA revealed that if the password reset goes wrong, the customer is four times less likely to complete the mortgage journey with the bank. That's an unexpected connection and one that was costing the bank money.

It's fixable too. Now, if you've started a mortgage inquiry and you have a password problem, the bank will reach out to you and solve your problem quickly, generating a positive customer experience that encourages you to keep your mortgage application on track.

Bieda and her team started tracking many other journeys like that. With CJA, they could see who started an operation to move money between accounts and ended up calling the call center 48 hours later. They could see where automation was failing and where customer service needed to step in.

Finding such journey glitches is one thing. Fixing them is quite another. BMO began to spin up cross-functional teams dedicated to improving specific journeys—for example, money movement. Those teams included people from multiple departments like analytics, digital, risk, fraud, process design, technology, customer care, and marketing. Their jobs had changed. No longer were they tasked with optimizing their own channels and functions regardless of the impact on others. As Bieda says, "They get up every day and work to build something that's truly customer centered."

While Bieda couldn't share specific financial results with me, BMO is clearly gaining ground. It has moved up in the J. D. Power rankings of retail bank customer satisfaction for large Canadian

banks. The bank has seen improvements on each journey it has been working on. Overall customer growth is up, which reinforces loyalty and contributes to significant improvements in profit.

Bieda anticipates connections between CJA and the virtual agents that will power the customer relationships of the future. "When you combine journey analytics, customer value segmentation, and the intelligence deployed through bots and AI, that will become our future. AI and machine learning will nourish the system. We'll have more dynamic interchanges, connect the customer to content in a more dynamic way."

At that point, the contact center becomes a dynamic source of intelligence in the customer ecosystem. It's where people end up when they're having a problem, and CJA can explain how that problem is happening and when and can even infer why. Companies can tap that intelligence to improve experience design across channels. They can leverage it in real time to make the contact center workers more effective. Eventually, they will use it to fuel automated virtual agents with insights that will get customers exactly what they need in any given moment to stay happy and loyal.

Bieda's advice is to develop a clear-eyed view of the world with customer journey analytics at the center, just as she has at BMO. "Create a vision of the journey, the fact of how customers actually experience your brand, not a myopic view or whatever you hope is happening. When you understand that, you can find out what's most important, where they're starting in digital and ending up in the contact center. You can honor what they are experiencing in a real way. The answers are always in the data."

Managing the contradictions at the heart of customer experience

Lori Bieda's experience points to exactly where and how companies can improve their results across all channels. Why hasn't everyone done what BMO has done?

Because while better customer experience (CX) ought to be the main goal when it comes to applying new technologies like virtual agents, it's much harder than it looks. The path to improved CX is potholed with contradictions.

While there is a vast amount of information now available about every customer you have, from their web clicks to their social media posts, there's no easy way to reveal which of that information is relevant in the moment.

Companies are organized to optimize the customer's experience *within* channels—such as their experience on an app or in a call center—but customers don't experience the company within channel silos. They experience it *across* channels.

Customer experience is the sum total of activities managed by multiple departments—marketing, sales, customer service—and is profoundly affected by everything from accounting rules to HR policy. But according to a survey by Russell Reynolds, only 39% of companies have an executive leading the charge across the company on CX.[1]

In every company, there are key points where the right intervention could reduce churn, create chances to upsell, and make customers much happier; the mortgage process at BMO is a good example. But finding those points in any given company requires plucking insights from a mountain of data and then coordinating action to address them across departments and channels.

The final contradiction is this: If all that customer data could be applied at the moment a customer calls or chats with a customer service agent, that agent could be much more efficient. But agents already deal with an overwhelming set of information

about each customer, so this set of insights becomes just one more source to manage.

How can you manage these contradictions? You need a radical new source of insight that can actually fuel your strategy. That's what CJA promises.

Ideally, the information from CJA could feed an automated system that would interact with the customer. I've already described that automated system: it's a virtual agent system.

In this chapter, I'll explain all the elements that make CJA an effective strategy right now—and how to get past all these contradictions that stand in the way. By the end of the chapter, I'll show you how CJA marries up nicely with the virtual agent systems I've been describing in the rest of the book.

Customer journeys are at the heart of customer experience

Customer journeys are an essential element in analyzing and acting on CX. They are the path a customer takes to get something done. A customer journey is the sum total of the experiences that a customer has as they move down the path to making a decision. That decision might be to get a mortgage, cancel a credit card, pick a university to attend, or buy a new pair of shoes. Some journeys are small, like resetting a password. Some are huge, like moving to a new home. But for any company, there are sets of journeys that are central to the experience of that brand. As you might imagine, journeys are intimately tied to the intents I've been talking about all along in this book—the things that customers actually want to do.

The traditional way that CX experts delve into customer journeys is with an exercise called journey mapping. The description I give here is based on Harley Manning and Kerry Bodine's customer experience book *Outside In: The Power of Putting Customers at the*

Center of Your Business, but it's not unique; people throughout the CX world do journey mapping in much the same way.

In a traditional journey mapping exercise, you start with a journey that you feel is important for a customer—say, reporting fraudulent activity on a credit card. Then you look at all the steps that happen along the way. For example, these steps might include noticing a questionable charge on a bill, seeking more detail on an app, looking up the customer service number on the back of the card, calling customer service, navigating the IVR system to get to an agent, reporting the fraudulent charge, getting assigned a case number, checking status online, and calling again to see when and how the charge was resolved. Notice that this journey crosses channels, with elements that include paper bills, the physical credit card, an app, an online site, and telephone interactions with a call center.

To understand the journey even better, the CX professionals will examine deeper elements of the ecosystem behind the experience, such as call center policies, IVR systems, billing systems, and app designs. They'll also seek to understand which parts of the ecosystem are working well and which are contributing to poor and broken customer experiences.

The objective is to understand everything within the company that makes a difference from the customer's perspective.

The focus on customer journeys is a step in the right direction, because it looks at experiences broader than individual touchpoints. As McKinsey's CX experts Ewan Duncan, Harald Fanderl, Nicolas Maechler, and Kevin Neher wrote in their report *Customer Experience: Creating Value through Transforming Customer Journeys*,

> . . . [F]ocus on identifying, understanding, and mastering the customer journey: the complete end-to-end experience customers have with a company from their

> perspective. That journey has a clearly defined beginning and end spanning the progression of touchpoints. Customers don't know or care who in a company owns the individual experience of billing, onboarding, service calls, and so forth. From their perspective, these are all part of one and the same journey. [2]

Journeys matter far more than touchpoints. McKinsey's consultants estimate that a company's performance on journeys is 35% more predictive of customer satisfaction than their performance on individual touchpoints. In a Salesforce.com survey of US marketing leaders, 78% said that creating a connected customer journey across all touchpoints and channels positively impacts revenue growth.[3]

In fact, even when touchpoint experiences are working, the full journey may not be. Imagine, for example, a customer (like the one in the credit card fraud example I described earlier) who interacts with an app, an IVR system, a call center, and a website in the course of solving their problem. For the sake of argument, assume that each of these channels has a 90% chance of delivering a satisfactory experience. The chance of the whole chain of interactions delivering satisfaction is 90% x 90% x 90% x 90%, which is only 66%. So while the executives in charge of each touchpoint imagine themselves to be doing a bang-up job with 90% satisfaction, the customer is only satisfied two-thirds of the time. This is why a focus on individual touchpoints is inadequate to understand satisfaction in journeys that cross channels.

My company's experience reveals that when customers are forced to change channels, Net Promoter Scores drop by at least ten points. It's worth analyzing which intents have a high correlation to positive and negative emotions and devoting extra attention to the customer journeys around those intents. For example, disputing bills is high stress for both the agent and the

customer. Acknowledge the importance of those journeys, and you might decide to have more experienced agents on standby for them or even to proactively contact people who seem to be having problems instead of waiting for them to call.

This matters to the bottom line. When McKinsey studied companies across the insurance and TV industries, it found a strong correlation between performance on the most important customer journeys and growth. A one-point improvement (out of ten) in performance on those journeys delivered an average of three percentage points of additional revenue growth.

So journeys and journey maps are necessary. But by themselves, they're not sufficient. The reason is that journeys and customers' reactions to them are in constant flux. Acting on them demands a system that analyzes journeys in real time: customer journey analytics.

Lots of data is not enough—customer journey analytics requires insight

As I mentioned in the preceding chapter, I recently visited an operation run by a cable TV company. The company was collecting vast amounts of information about each customer. Every time you changed the channel or pushed the volume-up button on the remote, the company had a record of it. What insights did the company get as a result of collecting all that data?

Nothing useful, from what I could see.

The aimless collection of masses of data in a capacious data warehouse doesn't make companies smarter. It just creates an IT project that sucks the company's energy. This is virtually the definition of "big data"—a collection of data so large that processing and analyzing it is a huge challenge in itself.

What's needed is a focus, not on collecting masses of data but on collecting the right data and connecting it through identifiers

across customers. As the CIO of the Boston Red Sox, Brian Shield, said,

> When you start focusing on the data, a very important aspect of digital transformation becomes clear to everybody in the organization: quality beats quantity every time. Until you can effectively harness the data, analytics is just a dream. In our case, there are more than ten different ways for someone to buy a ticket to attend a Red Sox game. This means we have ten ways by which an error can occur. Add to that the duplication of customer data, and you have the makings of a serious data-quality problem.[4]

In the McKinsey report I mentioned earlier, thinkers Ethan Hawkes, Kai Vollhardt, and Maxence Vancauwenberghe explain what it takes to make proper use of all this data:

> Today, vast amounts of interactions and opinions are captured in data: digital logs, social media and blogs, call recordings, frontline comments and logs, pictures, and videos. This represents a wealth of very specific information from which to pull insights to improve and better manage customer experience. In addition, data storage has largely become a commodity, and analytical tools . . . help connect these data to provide a view over time of each customer's touchpoints and to help businesses identify patterns and opportunities in these journeys on a nearly real-time basis.[5]

CJA is the science of turning that tracking information into insight, as BMO did for banking journeys. Forrester analyst Joana van den Brink-Quintanilha clarifies this in her report *The Seven*

Top Questions About Journey Analytics: "What makes journey analytics different from other types of analytics is the fact that it is steeped in the customers' point of view. It also combines customer behavior with time and stitches together data across silos, channels, touchpoints, databases, and systems."[6] This stitching together is how it's possible to surface insights from a mass of customer information from varied sources.

As Lori Bieda from BMO says, "Customer journey analytics is one of the most transformative areas of analytics that I've seen in the last 20 years. At its core is the supreme understanding of how customers consume brands."[7]

The stakes are very high. McKinsey estimates that across industries, "successful projects for optimizing the customer experience typically achieve revenue growth of 5 to 10% and cost reductions of 15 to 25% within just two or three years. Moreover, companies offering an exceptional customer experience can exceed the gross margins of their competitors by more than 26%."[8]

One place to focus is on complaints. Suppose you get 20,000 complaints every month. You might believe that those complaints are not coming because the mobile app has a problem, or the customer service center has a blind spot, or the website has a dead link. And those causes may be part of the problem. But further study may reveal that the problems are worse because of the journeys people undertake as they bounce around among all of these touchpoints.

You can identify the causes of these problems if you understand intent. If you can look back at all of a customer's interactions over a certain period—everything they did that touched the company—you can determine what they wanted to do. You can look at every page they clicked on, what emails they received and sent, what their accounts look like, how they were billed, when they talked to the customer care center and about what. You can determine where in the process they went wrong. Multiply that by

thousands of customers, and you can see just what problems and thwarted intents are undermining your customer relationships. Also, as BMO did, you can begin to reengineer those processes across channels to make those intents less problematic to act on.

Acting on customer journey analytics requires a cross-channel approach

If you spin up a CJA process to reveal where the problems are in your customer experience, *what are you going to do about it?*

Consider Lori Bieda's analogy comparing customers to flowing water. If you attempt to solve the problems that analytics reveals in a single channel—say, by improving chat-based customer service or fixing a website problem—you may solve one problem at the risk of redirecting the flow of customers into other places. If the problems simply flow from one channel to another, you've wasted your effort. For example, customer service metrics may improve but may do so at the expense of people getting frustrated at some other part of the process.

Organizationally, there must be a commitment to change. Often this happens only when companies designate an executive champion—often identified as the "chief customer officer"—and put that individual in charge of cross-functional improvements for the whole business. That authority extends to the creation of teams like the ones at BMO that are optimizing specific journeys, such as applying for mortgages or opening investment accounts.

Which problems are worth fixing? Analysts advising companies on strategy in this area suggest two approaches. In the top-down approach, a company looks at well-defined existing journeys (like the mortgages or the investment accounts) and uses CJA to identify places where they are failing. In the bottom-up approach, companies look in the data for signs of failures (such as nonrenewals or complaints) and track those back to determine

where the customer experience is going wrong. Many companies adopting CJA will incorporate both approaches. Basically, with these methods you can find what's going wrong in places you know are important and what's going wrong in places you didn't even suspect to be problematic.

McKinsey's analysis identified three ways in which these analyses pay off. They provide a clear view of what's actually happening in customer journeys, as opposed to what management imagines is happening. They pinpoint where the organization should invest its effort in making improvements. And they identify the root causes that lead to customer behavior, enabling the company to focus on better ways to engineer processes in the future.

Customer journey analytics successes

From these descriptions, it's clear that CJA is a challenge. You need the right data, the right tools, and the right corporate mindset. But is it worth it?

While this analytical approach to customer experience is relatively new, I found a number of companies that were putting it to great advantage. Telecom and wireless companies were among the leaders in taking advantage of CJA. Because of the high stakes for customer interactions and subsequent renewals (or defections) in telecom, they tend to find great potential for profiting from customer experience improvements.

- At a major US wireless company, CJA revealed how nine web pages generated 31% of the company's web traffic but also drove 56% of all subsequent calls to the call center. The carrier assembled a cross-functional team including digital, contact center, customer experience, and management staffers to solve the problem, much like the BMO teams I described at the beginning of this chapter.

Analyzing the journey across channels, the team was able to prioritize improvements across the web and the call centers. They're making progress toward their goal of reducing call volume by 15%.[9]

- A large US wireless provider is using CJA to deal with rapid increases in call volume generated by its subscriber growth. The resulting probabilistic analysis of each call now equips agents with information about what issues are likely to come up, what the subscriber already tried online, and which solutions will deliver the best customer experience. This application of CJA has reduced time spent per call by 67% and reduced call center volumes by 30%, even as it has improved customer satisfaction scores.[10]

- Sky, a UK TV service supplier, applies journey analytics in real time to allow customers with unresolved problems to "jump the line" and get routed more quickly to an agent. Similarly, a global telecom company identified renewal at the end of contracts as a crucially important customer journey. It created a queue in its call center for such customers and offered them special renewal terms. The resulting improvements in renewals added $20 million in annual revenue. [11]

- A South American wireless communications firm found a counterintuitive result: outbound phone calls the company made to suggest upgrades to customers who were way over their monthly plan allowance often backfired, triggering them to investigate competitors and sometimes, cancel their service. Journey analytics suggested a better option: targeting outbound upgrade calls only to customers with steady usage and less extreme overages.[12]

Utility companies were also early adopters because CJA helped them identify and head off costly customer service challenges.

- Eneco, a European power utility, discovered that customers' moves to new homes triggered high call volumes, even when those customers started their journeys on the website. The utility reduced calls and increased satisfaction by aligning web content with agents' call scripts and trained agents to answer questions about the online forms.[13]

- A utility found that when customers were requesting changes or extensions to billing arrangements, the key driver for satisfaction was not whether the arrangements were approved; satisfaction depended on how many calls the customer needed to make. When two or more calls were needed, customer satisfaction scores decreased by 15%. CJA also identified at-risk customers who had bounced between digital and phone channels to try to get the deal approved.[14]

I also saw some interesting analytics strategies with travel and retail companies, including some that had worked with my own company, [24]7.ai.

- We worked with Hilton to identify customers who don't follow the usual flow of an online booking. Hilton then pops up individualized guidance customized to what the consumer is reviewing. So far this effort has generated 450,000 chats with double the conversion rate and 97% customer satisfaction.[15]

- Online travel provider Xanterra used CJA to identify several different types of problems and opportunities. It figured out that its own email campaigns were inadvertently causing customers to call in wondering if their reservations had been cancelled. Analytics helped justify investments in a customer preference center to support targeted marketing campaigns, new call center technology that gives agents a complete view of all of a customer's bookings and data, and improvements in its guest satisfaction survey.[16]

- Office Depot tapped CJA to review 2.5 million customer interactions over nine weeks in web, email, and contact center channels. It discovered that 23% of customers who called the contact center had just visited its website, and 49% called within 30 minutes after placing an online order. In response, the retailer quickly made improvements in the online process for tasks such as adding a product, removing a product, or fixing a quantity. The result reduced costs and allowed agents to focus on calls to solve more complex problems.[17]

How customer journey analytics and virtual agents reinforce each other

Based on these examples, I hope it's clear that forward-thinking companies are now tapping CJA to find ways to improve their customer experience. But in the chapters leading up to this one, I explained how virtual agents were contributing to the same goal. How can these two approaches reinforce each other?

There are several ways to combine these strategies.

First of all, analytics, if properly implemented, can generate

real-time insight into what a customer is looking for. If a customer is following a path that many others have followed before, CJA will help identify that path and the intent associated with it. The result is that when that customer shows up in the call center or interacts by chat, the agent can have a far better idea of how to help them. That's what happened at both the utility company Eneco and the rapidly growing wireless operator I described in the previous section—they're using automated systems like the ones I described in chapter 5 to help customer service agents predict what customers are seeking. Even better, if you can predict a customer's intent based on patterns of customer behavior, you can train an automated chatbot to suggest solutions based on that customer's intent. CJA thus makes virtual agents and chatbots much smarter.

In addition to real-time interactions, analytics can help companies better design and invest in global changes that improve the customer experience. CJA is a great tool to identify hitches and opportunities in companies' most important customer journeys. Redesigning those journeys can help eliminate some of those calls and chats altogether and increase the likelihood that if a customer does end up in the contact center, you know exactly what their intent is and how to help them.

Finally, CJA also can help companies prioritize investments in customer experience, as the travel company Xanterra did. If you can use data appropriately to increase the probability that you can predict a customer's intent, you can then use that better prediction to justify investing in chatbots that will more frequently get customers exactly what they're looking for.

Customer journey analytics and virtual agents together will help you prepare for a future in which artificial intelligence makes your business not only more efficient but more responsive to customers. I'll share a peek at what that future looks like in the next chapter.

Part IV

THE VIRTUAL AGENT FUTURE

Chapter 10

CONVERSATION WITH CHATBOTS IS THE FUTURE OF BUSINESS

As you've seen throughout this book, there are plenty of obstacles between the present state of the world and a future in which virtual agents are commonplace. I've told you the story of virtual agents at companies like Avis Budget, Dish Network, and Nestlé. But I've also shared just how hard it is to effectively build such agents into smart speakers, how thorny it is to negotiate with platforms like Facebook and Amazon's Alexa, and how challenging it is for companies to get their own databases and interfaces set up properly to fuel such agents.

Even so, I can promise you that conversations with virtual

agents are the future of how companies will interact with customers. I was so sure of this that I bet my company, [24]7.ai, on the certainty that it would happen.

In this chapter, I'll describe why I'm so certain that this future is coming. Then I'll help you see just what that future is going to look like.

Why the virtual agent future is inevitable

The history of technological innovation shows us what it takes for a new technology to catch on and be successful. To succeed, a new technology needs all of the following:

1. It must work successfully and economically with existing technologies.

2. It must have powerful benefits for consumers.

3. It must have significant benefits for companies that want to connect to those customers.

4. It has to be able to hurdle obstacles, such as regulations, biases, or corporate architectures, that are blocking it.

How do these rules apply to virtual agents?

Virtual agents are workable now. You can buy an Amazon Echo for less than $50, and millions of consumers have already done so. You can push a button on your phone and ask Google Assistant to tell you who won the game or if your flight is on time. Natural language processing—in voice or text chat—keeps getting better as processors get faster, coders get smarter, and the systems themselves develop experience and grow. These systems connect to the real world—they can tell you if it's going to rain today, whether

the stock market went up, and when you have to leave to get to your appointment given current traffic conditions.

Virtual agents have powerful benefits for consumers. Consumers don't like to wait on the phone for answers, which is why they've adopted websites and mobile apps. Once virtual agent systems can answer most questions—and they're getting better all the time—people will learn to prefer them to apps or the web because there's no clicking or tapping necessary. They'll find it natural to converse with virtual agents, just as they do with other people. Once a virtual agent system can answer a question quickly and correctly, of course consumers will prefer it, because it's just less hassle. Unlike PCs and phones, virtual agents can safely get you answers in places like cars, kitchens, and living rooms where concentrating on a visual interface is dangerous or annoying. As I described in chapter 1, today's systems are based on the idea of "find me what I am seeking." Virtual agents, built on a paradigm of "get me what I want," are far more natural and powerful.

As I've shown with the examples in this book, these systems also have powerful benefits for companies. They promise an improvement over the inefficiency of training, paying, and dealing with the turnover of thousands of customer service agents. They can access customer systems more quickly and give more consistent answers. They scale up, and they work all day and all night and on weekends and holidays. They can also report where products or services are generating problems, allowing companies to continually improve their operations. They can make existing human agents more productive. Crucially, they finally make customer service part of a company's fully digital operations.

So why haven't virtual agents taken over the world already? Some hurdles remain. To analyze what's happening, let's review the challenges I described in the first nine chapters of this book and see how hard it will be for virtual agents to overcome them.

In chapter 6, I described some of the challenges that

conversational *platforms* have. Systems like Facebook Messenger and Amazon's Alexa stumble on the challenges of authenticating customers and ensuring that their data (for example, bank balances and media preferences) is kept safe and secure. But customers who go directly to companies' own applications bypass these problems. (That's why Bank of America's virtual agent, Erica, can work so effectively within the bank's own app, where authentication, privacy, and security are built in.) In the end, I think the big platforms will face limits on their capabilities unless they solve their authentication and privacy issues. Platforms like Amazon's Alexa and Facebook Messenger will have to connect you directly to companies and then stop listening in, as Apple Business Chat already does on Apple's iMessage. We already saw this dynamic in phone apps: Apple iPhones and Google's Android don't spy on the apps you run, because that would be a violation of trust. When these voice and messaging platforms make the same realization, they'll preserve privacy as well—or they'll fade in favor of other platforms that do.

In chapter 7, I described some of the corporate obstacles to virtual agents. The solutions to these obstacles will come from a powerful economic force: envy. If Bank of America's customers love Erica, then Chase has to match it or lose market share. If Comcast customers can order movies and debug connectivity problems by voice, Verizon and AT&T will have to catch up. Rising consumer adoption will fuel this envy. We've observed this before: when executives saw their kids using mobile apps of all kinds, the resulting mind shift caused those executives to be more open to building mobile apps. In the same way, as more executives and their families are talking to their phones and smart speakers and chatting on Facebook Messenger and WhatsApp, they'll begin to direct their companies to be present in those same channels.

In chapter 8, I described the challenge of corporate informa-

tion architecture—of systems in many companies that are not yet ready to hook up to virtual agents. But in the end, companies that don't adopt flexible architecture and APIs into their systems will fall behind on all technology channels, not just virtual agents. The march of progress and rising consumer expectations will force companies to open up and modernize their systems so that virtual agents can get access. The alternative is an increasingly inflexible and disconnected company that can't move at the speed its customers demand.

In the end, all the obstacles are just speedbumps on the road to the virtual agent future. When people *can* talk to devices and get answers, they *will* talk to devices to get answers. If they're talking, then companies will want to be there to provide the answers they're looking for. It's faster, it's easier, and it's cheaper than today's customer service channels. The technological and social currents are flowing in the direction of virtual agents. The question to ask now is this: What's downstream?

How the future will unfold

Humans' interactions with machines have always evolved in the direction of increasing convenience. Companies' strategies have evolved in parallel.

In the late 1990s, people increasingly moved online. By 2002, half of the US population were internet users.[1] Companies developed a *web-first strategy*, since they knew customers would probably get their first impressions of them via websites.

Fast on the heels of this trend, search began to become central. Google's algorithm dominated. Companies recognized that unless they appeared in searches, they were effectively invisible. This was the era of search engine optimization. Companies built their sites to be attractive to Google, a *search-first strategy*.

The first popular smartphone, the iPhone, debuted in 2007. By

2012, half of US mobile phones were smartphones.[2] Worldwide internet traffic from mobile devices surpassed traffic from computers in 2016. Companies once again changed their priorities, building apps and optimizing their sites for mobile viewing. They adopted a *mobile-first strategy*.

As I write this in 2019, conversational interfaces are just beginning to catch on. No one is ready to give up mobile phone apps and do everything with chat and voice. But the signs of a transition are already here. The rapid penetration of conversational devices, the fast-increasing capabilities of Alexa, Siri, and Google Assistant, and the explosion of text messaging platforms, from Facebook Messenger to Apple iMessage to WhatsApp and China's WeChat, tell us that conversation is here to stay.

A conversation-first strategy isn't warranted . . . yet.

But the day when conversation begins to dominate web, search, and mobile channels is coming. It may happen in the next few years; it may be farther off. But it *is* coming, and you need to be prepared for it.

The age of corporate bots is coming, and you don't want to be caught flat-footed when it gets here.

Your bot will become central to your brand

Right now, people's impression of your brand has a lot to do with what they see on your mobile site.

But as the conversation-first future arrives, a bot will be how people see your brand.

They'll want the answers to questions like these:

"How late is your store open?"

"Can you set up a test drive?"

"Do you carry sheets and blankets for my kid's dorm room?"

"How should my investments change as I approach retirement?"

These are questions that a conversational bot or virtual agent

can answer (or at least begin to answer) more easily than a website or app.

Are you ready for the day when a bot is a big part of your brand?

Consider the Butterball hotline skill on Alexa that I described in chapter 6. It's no coincidence that one of the voices of Butterball is Marge, an 81-year-old kindly grandmother type. Butterball wants you to think of it as a helpful, friendly brand that's ready to make you a hero on Thanksgiving Day, and Marge has just the right voice to communicate that image.

Mobiquity, which builds both mobile apps and conversational apps, has found that the two different kinds of apps demand completely different skills. The visual designers who are best at mobile app design *aren't* the best at conversational design. Mobile designers focus on using screen elements to get you a limited set of answers instantly. Conversational designers, by contrast, need to recognize hundreds or thousands of intents and create dialogue appropriate for them. A conversation is defined by back-and-forth, and that means it can include personality. If Butterball's Marge, KFC's Colonel Sanders, or Geico's Gecko have their voices embedded in bots that are ready to help you, that reinforces the way you think about the helpful values of those brands.

Today, every interaction becomes an element of how a brand tells its story—and brand storytelling is the heart of marketing. In their book *The Laws of Brand Storytelling*, Ekaterina Walter and Jessica Gioglio describe brand storytelling as "the art of shaping a company's identity through the use of narratives and storytelling techniques that facilitate an emotional response and establish meaningful connections." As they say,

> Brand storytelling done right is never self-absorbed; it is a dialog. It's human and real and relatable. It doesn't have to be dramatic or even funny, but it unites, sparks conversations, and puts people first.[3]

As Walter and Gioglio describe, brand storytelling can happen through a video, a tweet, a customer service interaction, or a public act. They recommend customizing and personalizing every brand's story based on the channels the brand is using. While they don't specifically call out chatbots, chatbots are an ideal (and increasingly important) channel for brand storytelling.

In a conversational scenario, speed to the answer is *not* the only brand value that matters. The customer's satisfaction with time spent becomes equally important. For example, now that banks have made it possible to do everything from paying bills to depositing checks from your phone, they've started making their branches and the staffers there absurdly friendly and helpful. They *want* you to come in so they can show you how nice and helpful they are. Capital One's branches have even been reconfigured to resemble cafes. Bank brands know that because you come into the branch so infrequently, it's their one chance to make a positive impression.

In the same way, brands will engineer their conversational interfaces to be as pleasurable as possible.

In his book *Digital Disruption,* James McQuivey suggests that the right metric for future brand success is the average number of minutes that a customer spends with that brand per day. More minutes means more chances to make a positive impression and keep the customer committed to the brand. In this analysis, a conversational interface that's positive and helpful and that reinforces other brand values becomes a crucially important attribute of every brand strategy.

Given the stakes, I expect an arms race to develop for well-scripted conversations. Just as brands now hire top directors to make striking commercials, I think the brands with the most at stake will start to hire the world's best storytellers to help script their bots. I can see the beginnings of this happening already; for example, Emma Coats, the "character lead" for Google Assistant, worked at Pixar on the animated feature *Brave.* As she told the

New York Times Magazine, "Pixar is all about finding an emotional reality in a car or a fish . . . So that's something we've really used with the Assistant."[4]

In the future, brands may find that, at the right price, Aaron Sorkin (*Moneyball*), Quentin Tarantino (*Pulp Fiction*), or Ben Stiller (*Zoolander*) will be ready to architect their brand conversations.

As the conversational interfaces dominate customer interactions, other interactive channels will become subsidiary. Websites, for example, could become much simpler, with information reflecting what the company has learned about you from your bot conversations. Actual customer service agents will be trained to use terminology and conversational tones that match what the company has paid for to make sure that real and virtual agents appear to be singing from the same hymnal.

In chapter 6, I described how Nestlé's GoodNes skill sets up a customized web page that updates itself as you step through a recipe. In the same way, your web page on Fidelity, DirecTV, or Tesla might reflect the conversations you've been having about finance, television programs, or driving directions. If a brand is listening, it's going to show the best face for you, the individual—and if you need something else, you can just ask for it.

Dancing with giants

When the web became popular, no one had overarching control over it. This created a relatively level playing field for companies trying to connect with their customers—anyone could easily connect with any site, with no gatekeepers.

Even though Google dominates search, site discovery online remains on a relatively level playing field—anyone can get to the top of Google's listings with relevant content.

And on mobile devices, even though Apple iOS and Google's Android are the platforms for app downloads, they don't

play favorites; it's easy to download and install the app for any company that you have a relationship with, or failing that, to visit its mobile website.

But when it comes to conversational applications, the level playing field is gone. It's true that you can build conversational interfaces into your site and apps, where you control the interaction. This is what Bank of America did with its Erica chatbot, for example. But that presumes that people want to start at your site or within your app.

As Amazon, Google, Apple, and Samsung's conversational platforms spread, they will become the "first ear" listening to any request.

For example, when you tell Alexa, "I want to order a pizza," it will determine which suppliers to connect you with. (When I recently tried to order a pizza with Alexa on my Amazon Echo, it attempted to place an order with Whole Foods, which, of course, Amazon owns.) As I described in chapter 6, the owners of these platforms have made no guarantees about whether they will gather data from applications and skills running on their platforms.

I doubt that Amazon is going to limit its retail ambitions to Whole Foods. It distributes video through Amazon Prime and sells apparel and shoes through its subsidiary Zappos. It has already acquired the online drugstore PillPack. Amazon's CEO Jeff Bezos owns the *Washington Post*. Looking ahead, the prominent financial analyst Gene Munster has even speculated that Amazon would buy Target,[5] and Amazon could very easily buy a travel supplier, like Expedia. If there are limits to Amazon's retail and distribution ambitions, they're certainly not visible.

This makes a difference to potential partners coveting a channel for conversational connections and commerce. A few will make the devil's bargain and live with Amazon potentially gating their access; others will look for alternatives that are more likely to offer a level playing field with guaranteed security.

What would this mean for conversational platforms?

Apple, whose current conversational platform, Siri, is less capable than Amazon's Alexa, could attract more partners with a more capable platform. Given Apple CEO Tim Cook's position on privacy, articulated in his speeches about the necessity to preserve the security and privacy of customers' data[6] and Apple's evenhanded, no-spying behavior with Apple Business Chat, Apple could win over both consumers and businesses who prefer a safer environment. It might need to beef up its technology by licensing additional capabilities from Microsoft's Cortana or other leaders in speech recognition.

Google is currently treading down the same path as Amazon, but it's far behind. If Google gathers customer data from its partners, it's unlikely to be a popular partner. It could take the no-spying pledge as Apple did and become a more viable option.

If Amazon continues to collect data from conversations and use it to benefit its own subsidiaries and projects, it may find itself in the crosshairs of the Federal Trade Commission (FTC), a US regulator that takes a dim view of monopolistic behavior on the part of platforms. Government regulators forced Microsoft to open up APIs in its then-dominant browser in 2001[7] and demanded reforms to how Facebook used data in its consent decree with the company in 2011.[8] It's conceivable that the FTC—perhaps based on new data-sharing regulations—could demand that Amazon create a level playing field and never collect data from third parties operating on its Alexa platforms. Such a decree would instantly make Alexa a preferred partner for the retailers and other suppliers currently nervous about working with it.

I continue to believe that it's far more important for companies to work on the back end: the mechanisms that they use to detect intents and deliver conversational responses, independent of the platform where they're delivered. If you've built that, you'll be in a position to deploy it on your website and apps and improve your

conversational capabilities based on the experience. Then you'll be ready to hook your application into Alexa, Siri, Google Assistant, or any other platform that emerges based on what your customers and your market demands and not be beholden to those platforms for access to your own customers.

Industry by industry, bots will determine leaders and laggards

Let's look back to past transformations and what they did to companies' competitive positions.

Few realized the importance of the web in the mid-1990s. But today, companies invest heavily in their websites and everything associated with them, because online is often their most important channel. Retailers need to not only sell online but also coordinate those online sales with what goes on in the store. Airlines and hotels compete partly on the ease with which you can make reservations online. Banks that don't offer online banking look obsolete. There is no industry in which an effective website and online strategy aren't a big part of a company's competitive position.

In 2008, apps were curiosities. Now they're crucial. But now banks, retailers, travel companies, cable operators, and every other kind of company imaginable compete on the quality and capability of their mobile apps.

We are at a similar competitive crossroads for conversational applications. As I write this, no one is demanding that every company they work with has a voice or chat application. But expectations are beginning to change. Already, most customer service sites offer a chat option, behind which may be a human—or a chatbot. All the popular music services, like Pandora and Spotify, offer Alexa and Google Home applications, because being shut out of those devices would mean spitting in the eye of the future.

Just as mobile applications spread from industry to

industry, I expect the same evolution to happen with conversational applications.

It will start with media. It's already mandatory that audio applications such as NPR, iHeartRadio, and music streaming services have an application on conversational platforms. I think all news suppliers will follow. The idea that you couldn't receive Fox News, CNN, or the *New York Times* on your home device will soon seem quite outdated.

Next will come companies offering high-demand services. Commerce will be difficult, as I described in chapter 4. But because customer service is so important to travel, financial services, and telecom companies, I expect them to invest in chatbots and have them up and working by 2020. You'll be able to check the status of flights, determine your balance, or solve problems with your mobile phone, internet, or television subscription. Once one supplier in a category has implemented these features, others will follow.

In retail, conversational commerce is challenging because it's so hard to select among thousands of choices—websites are better for that. But for replenishment, voice commands are ideal. If you need a ream of copy paper every few weeks, Staples will make it easy to get one.

The health care industry is an interesting case. Amazon has already invested in an Alexa health and wellness team,[9] and Jeff Bezos is backing a disruptive health care startup chaired by the deep medical thinker Atul Gawande.[10] A voice interface is ideal for answering simple health questions ("Can I take an antihistamine if I have high blood pressure?") or coaching people with chronic conditions ("Time to get up and take a walk now." "Have you taken your antidepressant today?"). I'd expect health insurers to invest in conversational applications to help their members suffering from chronic diseases such as diabetes, obesity, and Alzheimer's. If Apple enters this market—or enables others to—it could leverage the health data it is collecting from its smartphones and Apple Watches.

The authentication and privacy problems I described earlier in this chapter will be an obstacle for retail, travel, and financial services applications that covet transactional capabilities—allowing you to buy products from Whole Foods, for example, or send money through Venmo. But if you look far enough out, consumer demand and the competition among platforms will likely deliver solutions to these problems. By the 2020s, you'll expect to receive service and conduct transactions on voice platforms with every company that has a relationship with you, just as you now expect such companies to connect with you on their websites and apps.

As these capabilities emerge, expect suppliers in these industries to compete based on the quality and ease of their offerings. Just as Pandora and Spotify are competing today based on how well their applications work on Alexa, in the future, people will demand the greatest power and simplicity as they talk to their bank, their airline, their favorite hotel chain, or their retailers. If you can tell Hilton but not Hyatt to find you a hotel room in Palm Springs in January, then Hilton has a significant advantage. If Fidelity makes it easy to buy shares in the company you just heard about on NPR, it has an edge over Vanguard. Of course, if it's easier to order a pizza from Pizza Hut than from Dominos, that might make a big difference when you get hungry during the football game.

Companies that move early in these service-heavy markets will learn the new language of conversational service and make the necessary investments in figuring out technical, API, and privacy challenges. Others will find themselves at a significant disadvantage as customers increasingly develop habits with suppliers whose chatbots are capable and instantly available. Create a lead in these spaces and you'll gain market share, because your competitors will find it challenging to keep up with the effortless service you'll deliver.

There's one other advantage that the early movers in each

industry will have: data. Every conversation makes companies smarter about their customers. When you have a complete record of all of your customers' intents over time, you can map out their journeys and potential future relationship with your company. Every conversation is a communication generating data that your competitors are missing out on. As a result, every conversation will improve the strength of your connection with these customers.

Virtual agents will change the nature of work

In chapter 5, I described how bots and people will work together in the workforce of the future. I also said that by 2025, it will be unimaginable to work without help from bots.

What macroeconomic changes will this make in labor markets?

Drudge work has always been a target for automation. There used to be a category of worker called "laundress"—no one is sad that we're mostly doing our own laundry with machines now. "Computer" once meant a worker who performed arithmetic; now digital computers do that drudge work.

As for the work of serving customers, that's been shifting around for a while now. In the first decade of this century, millions of contact center jobs moved to lower-wage countries like India and the Philippines. These workers then began to shift from answering phones to chatting with text, in part so they could handle more conversations at once. These are not unskilled jobs; contact center workers need to manage interactions with multiple systems at once while juggling potentially unhappy customers. But as with laundresses and people working out math with pencils, the job of contact center worker is shifting as a result of virtual agent automation.

With virtual agents handling many of the common queries, the remaining contact center workers will need different skills. They'll certainly need empathy, because anyone who can't be

helped by a virtual agent is probably pretty upset. They'll need a more nuanced knowledge of corporate systems and policies, because they'll be dealing with the most complex questions that the virtual agents can't figure out. And, as described in chapter 5, they'll need to work closely with bots to get the answers to that trickier set of problems.

As a result of these demands, the contact center worker of the future will be a more educated type of worker. The required combination of sophisticated knowledge and empathy will demand the same skills as other knowledge-rich helping professions, such as nurses and teachers. Educational institutions will likely offer graduate certifications in customer services to help supply the training needed for these workers.

The future contact center worker may need other skills as well. A company attempting to stay competitive needs to keep maintaining and improving its virtual agents. Since the contact center workers will be handling the exceptions that the virtual agents can't handle, they'll be in the best position to identify new types of intents that the virtual agents could be programmed to address. I expect some of the next generation of contact center workers to specialize in programming, training, and scripting virtual agents and tweaking their algorithms to make them even smarter.

As AI and machine-learning tools become more standard, some contact center workers will graduate to being developers or script creators for bots.

The world of virtual agents and bots will also demand a set of narrative skills unlike any other type of programming job. I've already described how companies will employ the most talented screenwriters to set an overall personality for their bots. But at a more basic level, bots will demand the storytelling skills that are currently most common in copywriters, dramatists, and journalists. A new job description will emerge: conversational scriptwriter.

Just as game development sucked up talent from the movie industry and turned it to a new purpose, bot development will swallow up those with narrative skills. Those who best master this new medium will train others—and the bots themselves will provide feedback on which scripts are working most effectively.

In 2016, the US Bureau of Labor Statistics reported that 131,000 Americans had jobs as writers. By 2026, it's likely that at least that many people will be scripting interactions for virtual agents and bots.

People will be getting their own bots

Right now, terms like "Alexa," "Bixby," and "Google Assistant" refer to generic bots that are basically the same for everyone. But bots are capable of learning—when you tell Siri which of your contacts is your dad, it remembers for next time. By 2020, I expect a rapid and highly competitive market to emerge selling bots that become increasingly personalized to you, the user. (If you saw Spike Jonze's 2013 movie *Her*, in which a bot with the voice of Scarlett Johansson becomes the intimately personal assistant for a man played by Joaquin Phoenix, you got a preview into what this world would be like.)

The prospect of personal assistant bots—or personal agents—could dramatically shift the demands on the virtual agents that companies create. Instead of virtual agents interacting with customers, they may end up interoperating with those customers' personal agents. We'd enter a world in which information and transactions would be negotiated between these two types of bots.

I believe this type of interaction will depend on a set of bot-to-bot protocols that will allow bots to digitally connect and share information. There's a long history of such standards, including the set of standards that allows your web browser to share information with any company's web servers on any site you visit. It's

pretty much inevitable that a similar set of standards will evolve to mediate communication between bots.

These standards might reverse one of the most pernicious trends of our time—the closing off of the open web. In the '90s, thanks to the vision of Tim Berners-Lee, any browser could visit any site. Now people increasingly spend their time in walled-off sites and apps like Facebook, Amazon, TikTok, and WeChat. The internet has been replaced by a "splinternet" where ad-supported companies and their algorithms, rather than evenhanded standards, determine what content you see. But once we each have our own personal bot finding experiences for us, we're more likely to get access to a variety of content on a more level playing field, busting apart the splinternet silos.

Once the bot-to-bot standards become established, people will be able to have experiences like these:

- You want to change your hotel reservation. Instead of contacting the hotel's virtual agent directly, you tell your own bot the limits of what you're looking for (which days, what prices, what levels of quality) and let it come back to you with the best possible reservations.

- You want to buy a car. You tell your bot to set up test drives with all cars that meet a certain set of specs, and it uses access to your schedule to set up times with the local dealers for those car brands.

- You want to find a new restaurant with great vegetarian meals. You instruct your bot to find three-star restaurants with special deals in the next month. It knows, for example, that you love Indian food but don't like Szechuan. Your bot surveys online reviews, negotiates with the restaurants' bots, and sets up reservations for you.

- You want to watch television more cheaply. Your bot finds the advertisers who are most interested in reaching you based on your personal characteristics right now—your income, your desire to find a summer camp for your daughter, and your taste in wine and movies, for example. The bot searches across advertisers and identifies those most likely to pay to advertise to you, then brings that information to your TV suppliers, like Netflix or Apple TV. As a result of this ad deal that your bot has negotiated, you can watch TV cheaply and see ads better suited to your immediate personal needs.

Once a personal bot gets to know you, it will make personal recommendations all the time. Already, Google Assistant knows your schedule and recommends when you have to leave the house to make it to your appointments, accounting for real-time traffic reports. In the future, personal bots will tell you when to refinance your home, who is the best therapist for you right now, and how to change your workout schedule to accomplish your health goals. It won't tell you not to have French fries with that burger . . . unless you've instructed it to nag you about food. Depending on how much you want to pay, these recommendations could either include or exclude subtle suggestions based on payments by marketers (otherwise known as ads).

One of the most important negotiations your personal bot will have is with the personal bot of your significant other. If you're a Democrat and your true love is Republican—or if you like zombie movies and he likes romantic comedies—then your bot's recommendations and those of your partner's bot won't match up. Past couples had to deal with merging their album collections and figuring out what restaurants they both like; future couples will need to harmonize their Siris and Alexas to generate shared recommendations that won't create discord in your relationship.

The seamy side of conversational interfaces

Every technology innovation brings its own problems. Without the internet, we could never have so many data breaches. Social media vastly elevated the spread of fake news. Mobile device addiction has raised rates of teenage anxiety and depression[11] and increased the number of auto accidents.[12]

The internet and mobile phones have created far more good than the harm they have caused, but the harm is real.

So a responsible thinker has to ask: What are the potential downsides of virtual agents and chatbots?

Just as with email or social media, bots can be turned to malign purposes. That's a worrisome concept, because with artificial intelligence behind them, bots may evolve to be very good at charming people out of their bank account information, persuading them to vote against their interests, or manipulating their emotions. If you're on Facebook, you've likely received random friend requests from profiles that appear to be attractive and sexy single women or well-muscled, silver-fox ex-military types. They're fake friends, and they're there to try to create a fake relationship with you and get you to send them money.

Right now, these requests are easy for an intelligent person to spot and avoid because the profiles are clearly fake. But in the future, AI may make it a lot easier for such profiles to chat with you and to appear not only real but particularly attractive to you based on your personal tastes.

These sorts of risks have already led to a 2018 California law that requires all bots to identify themselves as bots.[13] I support this idea. No one should be confused about whether they're talking to a human or a bot. True, as I described in chapter 1, in many cases you'll prefer talking to a bot because it will be more efficient and make fewer demands on your emotions. You still deserve to know when you're talking to a bot and when you're talking to a person.

The other challenge is what happens when bots don't do what they're supposed to do.

We've already seen this happen. As an experiment, Microsoft launched a Twitter chatbot called Tay in 2016 to see what would happen if real people interacted on Twitter in a virtual conversation. Microsoft engineered the chatbot to learn to become a more effective conversationalist from its interactions. Unfortunately, racist and misogynistic trolls interacting with Tay rapidly taught it to interact in disturbing ways.[14] When your bot is saying things like "I f***ing hate feminists and they should all die and burn in hell," it has clearly gone over to the dark side.

Bias in algorithms is a serious problem, but with proper design, chatbot designers can ensure that their bots remain helpful and civil.[15] (In a typical bot design scenario, all of the answers follow scripts that are under the control of the designers.) But what happens when actual malign actors take control?

Instead of hacking websites, thieves could hack chatbots to encourage them to perform activities such as requesting people's passwords or social security numbers or sharing bank account information. Embedded in a conversational flow, such requests might seem natural—if you're chatting with your investment bot and want to make a transaction, you might not be surprised when it requests your social security number as an authentication method. To protect against such types of hacking, companies will need to prioritize security in their bot design and development protocols, just as they currently ought to be doing with their storage of customers' data. We'll also need to train consumers to be skeptical of certain types of requests in chat and voice interfaces, just as we educate them now on how not to get sucked into phishing emails.

Which bots will be most secure? Thus far, Apple and Amazon have not suffered any consumer data breaches. (People have cracked passwords on individual Apple iCloud accounts, and companies

using Amazon Web Services have lost data due to their own security practices, but as I write this, neither tech company has had a breach of the consumer data they store.) In the wake of Facebook data breaches, this discipline may make Apple's Siri and Amazon's Alexa appear safer than offerings based on Facebook Messenger, for example. Google has been relatively secure—its only breach was associated with the now shut-down Google+ social network—but as more people tell more things to Google Assistant, we'll see if the company can maintain a trustworthy reputation.

These levels of trust will become increasingly important because people are going to tell their personal assistants everything from how they want to move money around to where they're going on vacation to what they want to buy for Christmas. Once a hacker infiltrates a personal assistant, I expect the affected vendor to rapidly lose share, and the whole market to suffer a shock.

In fact, with the level of data that virtual assistants are collecting, current laws are going to be out of date. Among broadly implemented security and privacy laws, Europe's General Data Protection Regulation (GDPR) is the most stringent, requiring, among other provisions, that companies immediately make customers aware that their data is being collected and allow customers to request that all their data at a given company be deleted. Bots may actually help with compliance to regulations like GDPR, since they tap in to and integrate with the corporate systems that include a customer's data, the exact collection of information that GDPR applies to. Even so, I'd expect Europe, and later the US, to extend privacy laws regarding the protection of consumer data collected by corporate and personal bots.

As a safety feature, we may also see laws prohibiting bots from certain obviously problematic activities, like making medical recommendations that are normally best left to doctors. (Already, platforms like Alexa prohibit bots from asking for credit card information.) Laws restricting financial activities will annoy

consumers by restricting convenience, but they may be the only way to ensure these platforms remain safe and secure.

When everything can listen and talk back, the world will change

Despite the admitted challenges in getting the age of intent off the ground, I'm certain that it's going to happen—and change the world in a big way.

The security and privacy hurdles I've described, the difficulties with authentication, the challenges of working with big platforms—these challenges are all on their way to being solved. Why? Because that's what always happens when a technology makes things easier for consumers and more effective for the companies that serve them. The age of intent—a world where you can talk or chat with companies on almost any device you want—is on its way here.

This will challenge the very idea of interactive devices. Of course you'll talk to your computer and your phone and the smart speaker in your living room. But inevitably, you'll talk to your car as well (what better hands-free environment could there be?). You'll ask your refrigerator what recipes you can make with the food inside of it, suggest that your thermostat warm things up for your son when he gets home, and request that your TV lets you know when the score of the big game is getting close. All of these devices will be connected, and they'll all use voice as their primary interface.

For companies that sell anything from pharmaceuticals to travel, there is a choice. Those companies can participate in a future where understanding and anticipating the customer's intent—and acting on it—is a central part of the relationship they have with that customer. Understanding intent will enable companies to anticipate customers' needs and deliver powerful,

appropriate customer experiences at the moment they need to shine: when the customer contacts them. To make this work, those intents and responses will have to work in any environment where the customer may be asking a question, because when somebody wants to talk to you, you'd better answer.

We're at the very beginning of this profound transformation. It's hard to know just how fast it will get here, exactly what shape it will take, and how it will change the worlds of business and human interaction. But make no mistake: the age of intent is upon us. And unless you're preparing for it, you're going to be left behind.

ACKNOWLEDGMENTS

The Age of Intent came together as a book because of a broad team effort.

Companies are only now beginning to embrace the potential of virtual agents, chatbots, and artificial intelligence. As a result, we had to cast a wide net to find people with real, practical experience implementing these technologies successfully. That took time and research—a lot of it. We could never have completed that research and shared these companies' experiences without a lot of help.

Josh Bernoff was my cowriter on this project. Josh's guidance was invaluable throughout this entire process, from developing the outline to fleshing out the themes of each chapter to ensuring we met our deadlines. I can't thank him enough.

I'm deeply indebted to the people and companies that permitted us to tell their stories as case studies. These include Avis Budget, Bank of America, BMO, Butterball, Dish Network, HubSpot, IHG, Nestlé, Nordea, Optus, SEB, SiriusXM, and TGI Fridays.

The executives at these companies deserve enormous credit not just for their pioneering use of new technologies but also for their willingness to tell us about their experiences.

A committed team of people within my company, [24]7.ai, contributed generously of their time to help us make sure the book was rich with detail and focused on the right topics. Ian Bain shepherded the project forward for nearly two years, deftly managing internal and external resources to help us get to the finish line. Beth Brewer made a huge impact by dedicating her time and attention to the project and its associated research. I'm also grateful to content and technical experts who participated in multiple interviews across dozens of time zones, including Eddie Contreras, Andrew Hunt, Animesh Jain, Jens Koerner, Patrick Nguyen, Celene Osieka, Liz Powell, Vijay Raman, Adam Rubin, Angela Sanfilippo, Paul Sauer, Subha Sethumadhavan, Sanjiva Singh, and Gil Winters. The book benefited greatly from Scott Horn's content reviews, Dan Reed's client relationships, and Oindrila Hazra's analyst connections. And I must also single out my assistant, Shally Deng: without her graceful ability to sneak collaboration sessions in among my other responsibilities, this book would have never reached completion.

I'm also grateful to the analysts and other experts who generously contributed their time in educating us with unique market perspectives. These include Julie A. Ask, Van Baker, Seth Earley, Frank Eliason, Jessica Groopman, Daniel Hong, Fatemeh Khatibloo, Shail Khiyara, Sucharita Kodali, Rob Koplowitz, Craig Le Clair, Tina Moffett, Jeremiah Owyang, Mike Pace, Ty Rollin, Shyam Sankar, Ted Schadler, Joana van den Brink-Quintanilha, and Tom Webster. I'd also like to thank the experts at Forrester Research, Gartner, and Kaleido Insights for the valuable fruits of their research shared with us through research reports.

The team at Mascot Books/Amplify were the ideal partners to realize our manuscript as an actual published book. I'll single out

the ever-energetic Naren Aryal, the intrepid Kristin Perry, and the hard-working Daniel Wheatley, along with our copy editor, Kate Schomaker, for moving the book along to completion. I'd also like to thank the team at Cave Henricks for their help with promotion. I'll add a shout-out to Stephani Finks for her striking cover design. And thanks to Dan Gerstein and everyone at Gotham Ghostwriters for putting Josh and me together for such a productive partnership.

I want to thank my company's cofounder Shanmugam "Nags" Nagarajan. He has been my friend and partner on this journey for the last two decades.

I'm deeply grateful to the *New York Times* columnist Thomas L. Friedman for writing the foreword. I've greatly enjoyed all of our conversations over the years, and he has proven himself to be a singularly insightful commentator; his willingness to write such a thoughtful opening has added something very special and unique to what we've all created here.

Finally, I'd like to thank my wife, Marissa, for her final review and, as always, her support of my efforts.

I always strive to make companies more successful and their customers happier. All of these people have now contributed to that goal. It's an honor to be part of a crew this talented. I hope you enjoyed the fruits of our efforts.

ABOUT THE AUTHORS

P.V. Kannan

P.V. Kannan is the cofounder and chief executive officer of [24]7.ai, a leader in AI-driven customer experience software and services. P.V. cofounded [24]7.ai in 2000 to make customer service easy and enjoyable for consumers, and since then he has built a profitable company with more than 15,000 employees worldwide. [24]7.ai is redefining the way companies interact with consumers, helping the world's leading businesses attract and retain customers through a personalized, predictive, and effortless customer experience.

P.V. holds more than 30 patents (issued and pending), has written several articles that cover some of the key issues around AI and chatbots, writes regularly on LinkedIn with his posts

attracting thousands of views each, and has been featured in several books, including *The World Is Flat* and *That Used to Be Us*, by Thomas L. Friedman; *India Inside*, by Nirmalya Kumar and Phanish Puranam; and *Reinventing Management: Smarter Choices for Getting Work Done*, by Julian Birkinshaw. He has spoken at numerous industry conferences, including AI Congress and Forrester's CXNYC.

P.V. has been a pioneer in integrating technology with business process operations to improve all aspects of the customer experience. In 1995, his first company, Business Evolution Inc., developed the first generation of email and chat solutions. The company was acquired by Kana in 1999, and P.V. became part of the management team until he founded [24]7.ai.

P.V. is a recognized leader in customer experience, from dramatically improving contact center operations to developing a big data predictive analytics platform; to creating omnichannel solutions for the web, mobile, chat, social, and speech IVR; to innovating mobile-centric applications; and now to pioneering the use of AI in customer experience.

Josh Bernoff

Josh Bernoff is a bestselling author or coauthor of six books and recognized expert on writing, editing, and analytical thinking. His book *Writing Without Bullsh*t: Boost Your Career by Saying What You Mean* (HarperBusiness, 2016) is a definitive guide to business writing in the modern world. The *Globe and Mail* called it "a Strunk & White for the modern knowledge worker."

Josh blogs every weekday at Bernoff.com on topics in writing, analytical thinking, business, and politics. His blog attracted 2.5 million views in its first three years.

Josh's first book, *Groundswell: Winning in a World Transformed by Social Technologies* (Harvard Business Press, 2008),

written with Charlene Li, was a *BusinessWeek* bestseller. Abbey Klaassen, the editor of *Advertising Age*, picked it as "the best book ever written on marketing and media." His other books include *Empowered: Unleash Your Employees, Energize Your Customers, Transform Your Business* (HBR Press, 2010), written with Ted Schadler; *The Mobile Mind Shift: Engineer Your Business to Win in the Mobile Moment* (Groundswell Press, 2014), written with Ted Schadler and Julie Ask; and *Marketing to the Entitled Consumer: How to Turn Unreasonable Expectations into Lasting Relationships* (Mascot Books, 2018), written with Nick Worth and Dave Frankland.

For 20 years Josh was a principal analyst and senior vice president, idea development at Forrester Research, the elite technology research company. In that position he wrote over 100 research reports, gave speeches all over the world, and worked with Fortune 500 clients on business strategy. He appeared on *60 Minutes* and got quoted everywhere from the *Wall Street Journal* to *TV Guide*. The Society for New Communications Research recognized him as "Visionary of the Year."

Josh has lived in the Boston area for the last forty years.

REFERENCES

Chapter 1

1 "E-Commerce Will Make Up 17% of All US Retail Sales by 2022—and One Company Is the Main Reason," by Daniel Keyes, August 11, 2017, in *Business Insider.* See https://www.businessinsider.com/e-commerce-retail-sales-2022-amazon-2017-8.

2 "Forrester: US Mobile Sales Jumped 29% to $153B Last Year," by Robert Williams, April 11, 2018, in *Mobile Marketer.* See https://www.mobilemarketer.com/news/forrester-us-mobile-sales-jumped-29-to-153b-last-year/521076/.

Chapter 3

1 "DISH Named #1 in Overall Customer Satisfaction by J. D. Power," September 27, 2018, Press Release on Dish Network site. See https://www.dish.com/dig/news/dish-1-in-customer-satisfaction-j-d-power/.

2 "Customer Satisfaction Stagnates in Ominous Sign for Economy, ACSI Data Show," July 12, 2018, Press Release on ACSI website. See https://www.theacsi.org/news-and-resources/press-releases/press-2018/press-release-national-acsi-q1-2018.

3 Dimension data cited in "Transform the Contact Center for Customer Service Excellence," Forrester Research Report by Kate Leggett, February 23, 2018, footnote 2. See https://www.forrester.com/report/Transform+The+Contact+Center+For+Customer+Service+Excellence/-/E-RES75001.

4 "Transform the Contact Center for Customer Service Excellence," Forrester Research Report by Kate Leggett, February 23, 2018. See https://www.forrester.com/report/Transform+The+Contact+Center+For+Customer+Service+Excellence/-/E-RES75001.

5 "Contact Centers Must Go Digital or Die," Forrester Research Report by Kate Leggett and Art Schoeller, April 3, 2015. See https://www.forrester.com/report/Contact+Centers+Must+Go+Digital+Or+Die/-/E-RES122341.

6 "Transform the Contact Center for Customer Service Excellence," Forrester Research Report by Kate Leggett, February 23, 2018. See https://www.forrester.com/report/Transform+The+Contact+Center+For+Customer+Service+Excellence/-/E-RES75001.

7 "The Problem with Customer Service," July 29, 2015, in Consumer Reports. See https://www.consumerreports.org/cro/magazine/2015/07/the-problem-with-customer-service/index.htm.

8 "Artificial Intelligence from Salesforce Partner DigitalGenius to Boost KLM Customer Service," by Gil Press, October 5, 2016, in Forbes (online). See https://www.forbes.com/sites/gilpress/2016/10/05/artificial-intelligence-from-salesforce-partner-digitalgenius-to-boost-klm-customer-service/#5bbbf1a575e7.

9 "Unlock the Hidden Value of Chatbots for Your Customer Service," Forrester Research Report by Daniel Hong and Ian Jacobs, January 19, 2019. See https://www.forrester.com/report/Unlock+The+Hidden+Value+Of+Chatbots+For+Your+Customer+Service+Strategy/-/E-RES140452.

10 "Service Automation: Cognitive Virtual Agents at SEB Bank," by Mary Lacity, Leslie Willcocks, and Andrew Craig, February 2017, in the Outsourcing Unit Working Research Paper Series, University of Missouri–St. Louis. See http://www.umsl.edu/~lacitym/LSEOUWP1701.pdf.

Chapter 4

1 “Millennials Are Killing Chains Like Buffalo Wild Wings and Applebee’s,” by Kate Taylor, June 3, 2017, in *Business Insider.* See https://www.businessinsider.com/millennials-endanger-casual-dining-restaurants-2017-5.

2 “TGI Fridays CEO Reflects on New Brand Identity,” by Ron Ruggless, March 7, 2016, in *Nation’s Restaurant News*. See https://www.nrn.com/casual-dining/tgi-fridays-ceo-reflects-new-brand-identity.

3 “Conversable’s New Capabilities Empower Brands to Easily Deploy Bots across Voice and Messaging Channels,” July 3, 2018, Press Release on Cision PRWeb. See https://www.prweb.com/releases/2018/07/prweb15605119.htm.

4 “Chatbot Report 2018: Global Trends and Analysis,” by BRAIN (brn.ai), March 17, 2018, in Chatbots Magazine on Medium. See https://chatbotsmagazine.com/chatbot-report-2018-global-trends-and-analysis-4d8bbe4d924b.

5 “The Complete Guide to Conversational Commerce,” by Matt Schlicht, May 10, 2018, in Chatbots Magazine in Medium. See https://chatbotsmagazine.com/the-complete-guide-to-conversational-commerce-e47059293efa.

6 “Conversational Commerce: Why Consumers Are Embracing Voice Assistants in Their Lives,” by Jerome Buvat, Mark Taylor, Kees Jacobs, Amol Khadikar, and Amrita Sengupta, January 11, 2018, Capgemini Research Institute, p. 9. Downloaded from https://www.capgemini.com/resources/conversational-commerce-dti-report/.

7 “The Reality behind Voice Shopping Hype,” by Priya Anand, August 6, 2018, in *The Information*. See https://www.theinformation.com/articles/the-reality-behind-voice-shopping-hype.

8 “Simplifying Bookings with Messenger,” page on the Facebook Business site. See https://www.facebook.com/business/success/sephora.

9 “Two Months In: How the 1-800-Flowers Facebook Bot Is Working Out,” by Grace Caffyn, June 24, 2016, in *Digiday*. See https://digiday.com/marketing/two-months-1-800-flowers-facebook-bot-working/.

10 “The DoNotPay Bot Has Beaten 160,000 Traffic Tickets—and Counting,” by Khari Johnson, June 27, 2016, in VentureBeat. See https://venturebeat.com/2016/06/27/donotpay-traffic-lawyer-bot/.

11 “Political Bots Are Proving Exceptionally Effective at Registering People to Vote, Especially for Democrats,” by Michael J. Coren, October 19, 2016, in Quartz. See https://qz.com/810797/presidential-debates-political-bots-are-proving-exceptionally-effective-at-registering-people-to-vote/.

12 "Consumers Want Convenience, Not Conversations," Forrester Research Report by Julie A. Ask, Andrew Hogan, and Ian Jacobs, July 2, 2018. See https://www.forrester.com/report/Consumers+Want+Convenience+Not+Conversations/-/E-RES142249.

13 "Consumers Are Connected; Your Company Isn't," Forrester Research Report by Julie A. Ask and Mike Chirokas, August 13, 2018. See https://www.forrester.com/report/Consumers+Are+Connected+Your+Company+Isnt/-/E-RES143933.

14 "The Wired Society," May 1999, *Harvard Magazine*. See https://harvardmagazine.com/1999/05/wired.html.

15 "The State of Chatbots," Forrester Research Report by Julie A. Ask, Michael Facemire, and Andrew Hogan, October 20, 2016. See https://www.forrester.com/report/The+State+Of+Chatbots/-/E-RES136207.

16 "5 Technologies That Were Key to Alibaba Clocking $25.3 B GMV in 24 Hours," by Harshith Mallya, November 14, 2017, in Yourstory. See https://yourstory.com/2017/11/alibaba-global-shopping-technologies/.

Chapter 5

1 Graphic on Flickr by Gerd Leonhard, March 28, 2017. See https://www.flickr.com/photos/gleonhard/33545379262.

2 "The Future of Work: Intelligent Machines Whispering to Your Employees," Forrester Research Report by J. P. Gownder, July 17, 2018. See https://www.forrester.com/report/The+Future+Of+Work+Intelligent+Machines+Whispering+To+Your+Employees/-/E-RES142613.

3 "The Technology-Augmented Employee," Forester Research Report by J. P. Gownder, February 13, 2018. See https://www.forrester.com/report/The+TechnologyAugmented+Employee/-/E-RES125811.

4 "Gallup Daily: U.S. Employee Engagement" page on Gallup site, July 31, 2017. See https://news.gallup.com/poll/180404/gallup-daily-employee-engagement.aspx.

5 "AI Is Ready for Employees, Not Just Customers," Forrester Research Report by Craig Le Clair, March 27, 2018. See https://www.forrester.com/report/AI+Is+Ready+For+Employees+Not+Just+Customers/-/E-RES141543.

6 "'If Only HP Knew What HP Knows': The Roots of Knowledge Management at Hewlett-Packard," by Charles Sieloff, *Journal of Knowledge Management* vol. 3 issue 1 (1999), pp. 47–53. See https://www.emeraldinsight.com/doi/abs/10.1108/13673279910259385.

7 “Chatbot Case Study: Bupa, an International Healthcare Company,” by Chris McGrath, February 13, 2018, in Chatbots Magazine on Medium. See https://chatbotsmagazine.com/chatbot-case-study-bupa-an-international-healthcare-company-ff722974fea9.

8 “Confusion and Vendor Adolescence Stalls AI Innovation in Financial Services,” Forrester Research Report by Craig Le Clair, December 30, 2016. See https://www.forrester.com/report/Confusion+And+Vendor+Adolescence+Stalls+AI+Innovation+In+Financial+Services/-/E-RES136202.

9 “Confusion and Vendor Adolescence Stalls AI Innovation in Financial Services,” Forrester Research Report by Craig Le Clair, December 30, 2016. See https://www.forrester.com/report/Confusion+And+Vendor+Adolescence+Stalls+AI+Innovation+In+Financial+Services/-/E-RES136202.

10 “Allstate Business Insurance Agents Speed Up Quoting with Context Sensitive Help System,” on the Earley Information Science website. See http://www.earley.com/knowledge/case-studies/allstate%E2%80%99s-intelligent-agent-reduces-call-center-traffic-and-provides-help.

Chapter 6

1 “Facebook Hits New Peak of 1 Billion Users on a Single Day,” by Lucas Matney, August 27, 2015, in TechCrunch. See https://techcrunch.com/2015/08/27/facebook-hits-1-billion-users-in-a-single-day/.

2 “People Spend Almost as Much Time on Instagram as They Do on Facebook,” by Rani Molla and Kurt Wagner, June 25, 2018, in Recode. See https://www.recode.net/2018/6/25/17501224/instagram-facebook-snapchat-time-spent-growth-data.

3 “Messenger’s 2017 Year in Review,” by Sean Kelly, December 13, 2017, in Facebook Newsroom. See https://newsroom.fb.com/news/2017/12/messengers-2017-year-in-review/.

4 “Facebook Messenger Passes 300,000 Bots,” by Khari Johnson, May 1, 2018, in VentureBeat. See https://venturebeat.com/2018/05/01/facebook-messenger-passes-300000-bots/.

5 “WhatsApp Monthly Active Users Hit 1.5 Billion, 60 Billion Messages Sent Each Day,” by Indo Asian New Service, February 2, 2018, in Gadgets360. See https://gadgets.ndtv.com/apps/news/whatsapp-monthly-active-users-2018-1-5-billion-60-billion-messages-sent-per-day-300-million-whatsapp-1807232.

6 “Apple Users Send 200,000 iMessages Every Second” by Luke Dormehl, February 15, 2016, in Cult of Mac. See https://www.cultofmac.com/412432/apple-users-send-200000-imessages-every-second/.

7 “Facebook Messenger Passes 300,000 Bots,” by Khari Johnson, May 1, 2018, in VentureBeat. See https://venturebeat.com/2018/05/01/facebook-messenger-passes-300000-bots/.

8 “Amazon Says 100 Million Alexa Devices Have Been Sold—What’s Next?,” by Dieter Bonn, January 4, 2019, in The Verge. See https://www.theverge.com/2019/1/4/18168565/amazon-alexa-devices-how-many-sold-number-100-million-dave-limp.

9 “The Smart Audio Report,” NPR and Edison Research, Spring 2018. Downloaded from https://www.nationalpublicmedia.com/smart-audio-report/latest-report/.

10 “Alexa Is Right Up There with Mom, Dad and Cat,” NPR, Morning Edition, October 18, 2018. See https://www.npr.org/2018/10/18/658376612/alexa-is-right-up-there-with-mom-dad-and-cat.

11 “Advertisers Are Finding New Places for Ads with the Rise of Voice Technology,” by John Trimble, January 25, 2018, in Recode. See https://www.recode.net/2018/1/25/16929030/voice-interface-google-amazon-echo-assistant-advertising-audio-brand-platform.

12 “IFA 2018: Alexa Devices Continue Expansion into New Categories and Use Cases,” by Ted Karczewski, September 1, 2018, on Alexa Blogs. See https://developer.amazon.com/blogs/alexa/post/85354e2f-2007-41c6-b946-5a73784bc5f3/ifa-2018-alexa-devices-continue-expansion-into-new-categories-and-use-cases.

13 “Google Home & Assistant Stats,” web page on Voicebot.ai. See https://voicebot.ai/google-home-google-assistant-stats/.

14 “2018 Mobile and New Technology Priorities for Marketers,” Forrester Research Report by Thomas Husson, February 23, 2018. See https://www.forrester.com/report/2018+Mobile+And+New+Technology+Priorities+For+Marketers/-/E-RES139575.

15 “Plan for Success in Conversational Computing,” Forrester Research Report by Rob Koplowitz and Andrew Hogan, October 26, 2017. See https://www.forrester.com/report/Plan+For+Success+In+Conversational+Computing/-/E-RES138136.

16 “Takes Too Long to Accomplish Anything,” by John T., September 22, 2017, review of AMEX skill on Amazon.com. See https://www.amazon.com/gp/customer-reviews/R30EEJGNLTNAXD.

17 “Give Your Brand a Voice—Literally,” Forrester Research Report by Dipanjan Chatterjee, July 23, 2018. See https://www.forrester.com/report/Give+Your+Brand+A+Voice+Literally/-/E-RES141752.

18 “Yes, Facebook Is Reading the Messages You Send through Messenger,” by Lulu Chang, April 5, 2018, in Digital Trends. See https://www.digitaltrends.com/social-media/facebook-reads-messenger-messages/.

19 “It Turns Out That Facebook Could in Fact Use Data Collected from Its Portal In-Home Video Device to Target You with Ads,” by Kurt Wagner, October 16, 2018, in Recode. See https://www.recode.net/2018/10/16/17966102/facebook-portal-ad-targeting-data-collection.

20 “Google Home Is Playing Audio Ads for Beauty and the Beast,” by Chris Welch, March 16, 2017, in The Verge. See https://www.theverge.com/circuitbreaker/2017/3/16/14948696/google-home-assistant-advertising-beauty-and-the-beast.

21 “Burger King’s New Ad Forces Google Home to Advertise the Whopper,” by Jacob Kastrenakes, April 12, 2017, in The Verge. See https://www.theverge.com/2017/4/12/15259400/burger-king-google-home-ad-wikipedia.

22 “May A.I. Help You,” by Clive Thompson, November 14, 2018, in the *New York Times Magazine*. See https://www.nytimes.com/interactive/2018/11/14/magazine/tech-design-ai-chatbot.html.

23 “Join the Conversation to Build Customer Relationships,” Forrester Research Report by Thomas Husson, October 15, 2018. See https://www.forrester.com/report/Join+The+Conversation+To+Build+Customer+Relationships/-/E-RES137580.

24 “62 Percent of Alexa Skills Have No Ratings, but 4 Have over 1,000,” by Bret Kinsella, September 13, 2017, in Voicebot.ai. See https://voicebot.ai/2017/09/13/62-percent-alexa-skills-no-ratings-4-1000/.

25 “Complete Transcript, Video of Apple CEO Tim Cook’s EU Privacy Speech,” by Jonny Evans, October 24, 2018, in *ComputerWorld*. See https://www.computerworld.com/article/3315623/security/complete-transcript-video-of-apple-ceo-tim-cooks-eu-privacy-speech.html.

Chapter 7

1 “Unlock the Hidden Value of Chatbots for Your Customer Service Strategy,” Forrester Research Report by Daniel Hong and Ian Jacobs, January 19, 2018. See https://www.forrester.com/report/Unlock+The+Hidden+Value+Of+Chatbots+For+Your+Customer+Service+Strategy/-/E-RES140452.

2 "'Shoot Me a Text:' Why Millennials Prefer Text Over Talk," May 5, 2016, in Open Market Blog. See https://www.openmarket.com/blog/millennials-prefer-text-over-talk/.

3 "The Communications Market 2016," by Ofcom, p. 144. Downloaded from https://www.ofcom.org.uk/__data/assets/pdf_file/0026/26648/uk_telecoms.pdf.

4 "The Death of Voice: Mobile Phone Calls Now 50 Per Cent Shorter," by Andrew Orlowski, January 30, 2013, in *The Register*. See https://www.theregister.co.uk/2013/01/30/mobile_phone_calls_shorter/.

Chapter 8

1 "The New Moats," by Jerry Chen, April 24, 2017, in Greylock Partners on Medium. See https://news.greylock.com/the-new-moats-53f61aeac2d9.

2 "AI Readiness: Five Areas Businesses Must Prepare for Success in Artificial Intelligence," Kaleido Insights Report by Jessica Groopman, September 2018, p. 37. Downloaded from https://www.kaleidoinsights.com/order-reports/artificial-intelligence-ai-readiness/.

3 "Hidden Technical Debt in Machine Learning Systems," by D. Sculley et al., Google Inc. Downloaded from https://papers.nips.cc/paper/5656-hidden-technical-debt-in-machine-learning-systems.pdf.

4 "There's No AI (Artificial Intelligence) without IA (Information Architecture)," by Seth Earley, March 25, 2016, in InfoQ. See https://www.infoq.com/articles/artificial-intelligence#anch146294.

5 "What Is Digital Transformation? A Necessary Disruption," by Clint Boulton, December 3, 2018, in CIO. See https://www.cio.com/article/3211428/digital-transformation/what-is-digital-transformation-a-necessary-disruption.html.

6 "Digital Rewrites the Rules of Business," Forrester Research Report by Ted Schadler and Nigel Fenwick, April 27, 2017. See https://www.forrester.com/report/Digital+Rewrites+The+Rules+Of+Business/-/E-RES137784.

7 "Journalism That Stands Apart," report of the 2020 group, January 2017, in the *New York Times*. See https://www.nytimes.com/projects/2020-report/index.html.

Chapter 9

1 "Why Your Company Needs a Chief Customer Officer," by Chris Davis, Alex Kazaks, and Alfonso Pulido, October 12, 2016, on Forbes website. See https://www.forbes.com/sites/mckinsey/2016/10/12/why-your-company-needs-a-chief-customer-officer/#1776e89049d7.

2 "Customer Experience: Creating Value through Transforming Customer Journeys," McKinsey and Company, Winter 2016, p. 4. Downloaded from https://www.mckinsey.com/business-functions/marketing-and-sales/our-insights/customer-experience-creating-value-through-transforming-customer-journeys.

3 "Fourth Annual State of Marketing: Insights and Trends from 3,500 Global Marketing Leaders," Salesforce Research, 2017, p. 28. Downloaded from https://www.salesforce.com/form/pdf/2017-state-of-marketing.jsp.

4 "Moneyball II," by Brian Shields, July 14, 2016, in HCL Technologies Straight Talk. See https://straighttalk.hcltech.com/moneyball-ii.

5 "Customer Experience: Creating Value through Transforming Customer Journeys," McKinsey and Company, Winter 2016, p. 33. Downloaded from https://www.mckinsey.com/business-functions/marketing-and-sales/our-insights/customer-experience-creating-value-through-transforming-customer-journeys.

6 "The Seven Top Questions about Journey Analytics," Forrester Research Report by Joana van den Brink-Quintanilha, September 14, 2017. See https://www.forrester.com/report/The+Seven+Top+Questions+About+Journey+Analytics/-/E-RES136653.

7 "Customer Journey Analytics: Finding the Key Moments That Win or Lose a Customer," by Stannie Holt, July 14, 2017, in Opentext Blogs. See https://blogs.opentext.com/customer-journey-analytics-finding-key-moments-win-lose-customer/.

8 "Customer Experience: Creating Value through Transforming Customer Journeys," McKinsey and Company, Winter 2016, p. 4. Downloaded from https://www.mckinsey.com/business-functions/marketing-and-sales/our-insights/customer-experience-creating-value-through-transforming-customer-journeys.

9 "Answering the Call: The Subtle Art of Reducing Customer Call Volume," by Addison Howard, February 28, 2017, in Clickfox blog. See https://blog.clickfox.com/answering-the-call-the-subtle-art-of-reducing-customer-call-volume.

10 "2017 Retail, Wholesale, and Distribution Industry Outlook," Deloitte Center for Industry Insights, pp. 6–7. Downloaded from https://www2.deloitte.com/content/dam/Deloitte/us/Documents/consumer-business/us-cb-retail-distribution-outlook-2017.pdf.

11 "Brief: Learning from Three Early Adopters of Customer Journey Analytics," Forrester Research Report by Joana van den Brink-Quintanilha and Tina Moffett, May 2, 2016. See https://www.forrester.com/report/Brief+Learning+From+Three+Early+Adopters+Of+Customer+Journey+Analytics/-/E-RES132088.

12 "The Journey Analytics Road Map: From Start to Scale," Forrester Research Report by Joana van den Brink-Quintanilha and Alex Causey, July 11, 2017. See https://www.forrester.com/report/The+Journey+Analytics+Road+Map+From+Start+To+Scale/-/E-RES132085.

13 "Brief: Learning from Three Early Adopters of Customer Journey Analytics," Forrester Research Report by Joana van den Brink-Quintanilha and Tina Moffett, May 2, 2016. See https://www.forrester.com/report/Brief+Learning+From+Three+Early+Adopters+Of+Customer+Journey+Analytics/-/E-RES132088.

14 "Customer Experience: Creating Value through Transforming Customer Journeys," McKinsey and Company, Winter 2016, p. 34. Downloaded from https://www.mckinsey.com/business-functions/marketing-and-sales/our-insights/customer-experience-creating-value-through-transforming-customer-journeys.

15 "The Journey Analytics Road Map: From Start to Scale," Forrester Research Report by Joana van den Brink-Quintanilha and Alex Causey, July 11, 2017. See https://www.forrester.com/report/The+Journey+Analytics+Road+Map+From+Start+To+Scale/-/E-RES132085.

16 "Brief: Learning from Three Early Adopters of Customer Journey Analytics," Forrester Research Report by Joana van den Brink-Quintanilha and Tina Moffett, May 2, 2016. See https://www.forrester.com/report/Brief+Learning+From+Three+Early+Adopters+Of+Customer+Journey+Analytics/-/E-RES132088.

17 "The Journey Analytics Road Map: From Start to Scale," Forrester Research Report by Joana van den Brink-Quintanilha and Alex Causey, July 11, 2017. See https://www.forrester.com/report/The+Journey+Analytics+Road+Map+From+Start+To+Scale/-/E-RES132085.

Chapter 10

1 "United States Internet Users," web page on Internet Live Stats. Data from data by International Telecommunication Union (ITU), World Bank, and United Nations Population Division. See http://www.internetlivestats.com/internet-users/us/.

2 "US Smartphone Penetration Surpassed 80 Percent in 2016," by Adam Lella, February 3, 2017, in Comscore. See https://www.comscore.com/Insights/Blog/US-Smartphone-Penetration-Surpassed-80-Percent-in-2016.

3 *The Laws of Brand Storytelling: Win—and Keep—Your Customers' Hearts and Minds,* by Ekaterina Walter and Jessica Gioglio (McGraw-Hill Education, 2019), p. 4.

4 "May A.I. Help You," by Clive Thompson, November 14, 2018, in the *New York Times Magazine.* See https://www.nytimes.com/interactive/2018/11/14/magazine/tech-design-ai-chatbot.html.

5 "Commentary: 3 Reasons Amazon Will Buy Target This Year," by Gene Munster, January 15, 2018, in Fortune. See http://fortune.com/2018/01/05/amazon-target-buy-walmart-whole-foods/.

6 "Complete Transcript, Video of Apple CEO Tim Cook's EU Privacy Speech," by Jonny Evans, October 24, 2018, in *ComputerWorld.* See https://www.computerworld.com/article/3315623/security/complete-transcript-video-of-apple-ceo-tim-cooks-eu-privacy-speech.html.

7 *World War 3.0: Microsoft and Its Enemies* by Ken Auletta (Random House, 2001), p. 380.

8 "Facebook Settles FTC Charges That It Deceived Consumers by Failing to Keep Privacy Promises," November 29, 2011, News Release, Federal Trade Commission. See https://www.ftc.gov/news-events/press-releases/2011/11/facebook-settles-ftc-charges-it-deceived-consumers-failing-keep.

9 "Amazon Is Building a 'Health & Wellness' Team within Alexa as It Aims to Upend Health Care," by Eugene Kim and Christina Farr, May 10, 2018, in CNBC. See https://www.cnbc.com/2018/05/10/amazon-is-building-a-health-and-wellness-team-within-alexa.html.

10 "How Atul Gawande Landed Perhaps the Most Extraordinary (or Impossible) Job in Health Care," by Rick Berke, June 25, 2018, in Stat News. See https://www.statnews.com/2018/06/25/how-atul-gawande-landed-extraordinary-impossible-job/.

11 "Helping Teens Turn Off in a World That's 'Always On': The Links between Technology and Depression," by Donna Vickroy, December 22, 2017, in *Chicago Tribune*. See https://www.chicagotribune.com/suburbs/daily-southtown/news/ct-sta-teens-depression-technology-st-1220-20171221-story.html.

12 "Cell Phones Are Causing More and More Car Crashes," by Christopher Woody, May 31, 2015, in *Business Insider*. See https://www.businessinsider.com/cell-phones-causing-car-crashes-and-deaths-2015-5.

13 "A California Law Now Means Chatbots Have to Disclose They're Not Human," by Dave Gershgorn, October 3, 2018, in Quartz. See https://qz.com/1409350/a-new-law-means-californias-bots-have-to-disclose-theyre-not-human/.

14 "Twitter Taught Microsoft's AI Chatbot to Be a Racist A**hole in Less Than a Day," by James Vincent, March 24, 2016, in The Verge. See https://www.theverge.com/2016/3/24/11297050/tay-microsoft-chatbot-racist.

15 "Biased Algorithms Are Everywhere, and No One Seems to Care," by Will Knight, July 12, 2017, in *MIT Technology Review*. See https://www.technologyreview.com/s/608248/biased-algorithms-are-everywhere-and-no-one-seems-to-care/.

INDEX

B

C

H

I

J

K

L

M

N

O

P

Q

R

S

T

U

V

W

X

Y

Z

S0-BCR-858